# Financial services and the consumer

The growth in the numbers of financial service consumers in Britain in recent years has been remarkable. Yet the topic has received little attention. *Financial Services and the Consumer* fills an important gap by considering directly why this increase has occurred.

The volume presents a critical assessment of the strategies employed by financial institutions to create and maintain consumer demand for their products, especially though marketing, product development and branding. Dawn Burton also looks at the ways financial consumers have learned to 'play the system', resulting in conflict with financial services producers.

The discussion is placed in the wider context of public policy, consumer action groups, and social and cultural change. A particular focus is on the support given to the consumer against the producer through legislative changes in the 1980s, the introduction of the Financial Ombudsmen schemes and the activities of consumer groups. The book concludes by critically evaluating how far power relations within the producer–consumer relationship have actually changed in the financial service sector.

Drawing on recent examples of consumer financial behaviour in Britain, this book is a valuable insight into a topic of considerable significance. It will appeal to financial service practitioners and students in a range of social science and management disciplines.

**Dawn Burton** is a Lecturer in the Faculty of Social Sciences at the University of Sheffield and an Honorary Research Associate in the Sociology Department at Lancaster University.

# Financial services and the consumer

## Dawn Burton

London and New York

332.109
B97f

First published 1994
by Routledge
11 New Fetter Lane, London EC4P 4EE

Simultaneously published in the USA and Canada
by Routledge
29 West 35th Street, New York, NY 10001

© 1994 Dawn Burton

Typeset in Times by
NWL Editorial Services, Langport, Somerset

Printed in Great Britain by
Mackays of Chatham PLC, Chatham, Kent

*British Library Cataloguing in Publication Data*
A catalogue record for this book is available from the British
Library

ISBN 0–415–09961–7
ISBN 0–415–09962–5 (pbk)

*Library of Congress Cataloguing in Publication Data*
Burton, Dawn, 1961–
　　Financial services and the consumer / Dawn Burton.
　　　p. cm.
　　Includes bibliographical references (p.　) and index.
　　ISBN 0–415–09961–7.　ISBN 0–415–09962–5 (pbk.)
　1. Financial services industry – Great Britain.　2. Financial
services industry.　3. Consumers' preferences – Great
Britain.　4. Consumers' preferences.　I. Title.
HG186.G7B86　1994　　　　　　　　　　　93–44350
332.1′0941 – dc20　　　　　　　　　　　　　CIP

*For my precious son Wesley who makes life worthwhile*

# Contents

# Tables

# Acknowledgements

This book is based on my PhD thesis which I undertook in the Department of Sociology at Lancaster University, with financial support from the Economic and Social Research Council (R00428924034). I wish to thank my supervisors John Urry and Alan Warde for their assistance during the period of the research. Thanks must also go to the secretarial staff in the department, especially Maeve, who helped out along the way. I also wish to thank Nick Carter and Margaret Bayman for their friendship and considerable emotional support during the writing of the book. Finally, I am indebted to my wonderful, patient and loving son, Wesley, who amused himself for hours on end while his mum prepared the manuscript. I now have time to play!

*Dawn Burton*
*Lancaster*

# Chapter 1

# Introduction

The consumption of financial services has exhibited an extraordinary increase in Britain in recent years, yet the topic has received little extensive attention. In the early 1990s, over 90 per cent of the adult population in Britain were financial service consumers (Association of Payment Clearing Services 1992). There were periods during the 1980s when the clearing banks were in the unbelievable position of lending more to personal sector consumers than industry (British Bankers' Association 1993)! Buying goods and services on credit was no longer a shameful admission of poverty. As Leadbeater (1988: 14) has indicated, 'Under Thatcherism the credit card has become the symbol of citizenship, the entrance ticket to the consumer society.' The days when the possession of a financial service account was an exclusive preserve of the middle class have well and truly disappeared.

Since the vast majority of the adult population in Britain are financial service consumers, they have a vested interest in the way banks, building societies and insurance companies relate to their account and policy holders. This has led to a more critical evaluation of the way in which financial institutions treat their customers, and to discussions about what the 'proper' role of financial institutions should be. The image of financial institutions as being solid, stable and guardians of the nation's wealth, took a battering in Britain during the 1980s. The Third World debt crisis, appalling decisions in corporate banking and several major financial scandals, did little to repair the faltering reputation of financial institutions in the eyes of consumers.

The mass media has had an important part to play in demystifying the activities of financial institutions. The number of newspaper articles, radio and television programmes geared to providing consumer advice and guidance has increased considerably, and provides a measure of popular interest in financial affairs in Britain. Consumer groups such as the National Consumer Council and the Consumers' Association have also kept the consumer interest high on the agenda in the financial services sector throughout the 1980s and 1990s. The more complex financial services products have become, the more opportunity there has been for problems to occur. The media has not been slow to divulge the misdemeanours of financial institutions. Headlines such as 'Victims of the cashcard' and 'New banking code faces a mauling by consumers' are every day occurrences in 1990s Britain. These sentiments have been apparent despite several rounds of legislation which attempted to provide financial service consumers with extended freedom of choice and increased levels of protection. Financial institutions are well aware of the effects of bad publicity on business, and there have been occasions when they have questioned whether some of the accusations have been merited. For example, a recent article in the National Westminster Bank Quarterly Review posed the question, 'Don't Shoot the Messenger: Do Banks Deserve the Recent Adverse Publicity?' (Chrystal 1992).

The way financial service institutions have interacted with their consumers raises wider fundamental questions about the relationship between producers and consumers in advanced, capitalist societies. In the 1980s and 1990s, there was a great deal of debate among social scientists on the issue of consumption and consumerism. Many commentators advocated the arrival of 'new times', with the emphasis on individualism, consumption and consumer choice (Hall 1988; Leadbeater 1988). The notions of the 'enterprising' and 'sovereign' consumer are concepts which have gained considerable currency in recent years. A pivotal assumption on which many of the theories of consumer sovereignty rest is that advanced, industrial societies have witnessed a movement from mass to post-Fordist, individualised consumption (Harvey 1989; Burrows and Marsh 1992).

Urry (1990) has described mass consumption as a period when individual producers dominated particular markets, consumer choice was limited, and producers rather than consumers were dominant. Post-Fordist consumption is presented as a radical departure from mass consumption:

> consumption rather than production is dominant as consumer expenditure further increases as a proportion of national income; new forms of credit permitting consumer expenditure to rise, so producing high levels of indebtedness; much greater differentiation of purchasing patterns by different market segments; greater volatility of consumer preferences; the growth of a consumers' movement and the

'politicing' of consumption; reaction of consumers against being part of a 'mass' and the need for producers to be much more consumer driven, especially in the case of service industries and those publicly owned; the development of many more products each of which has a shorter life.

(Urry 1990: 277)

Furthermore, Abercrombie (1991) has argued that as a society, we are moving away from a scenario where strong producer cultures dominate and control passive consumers, to a position where the opposite is true. He believes producers have lost, or are losing, much of their social power and authority as producers. Under these conditions, consumers' aspirations run ahead of producers' ability to satisfy them. Successful companies will be the ones which constantly adapt to consumer choice and taste.

Whether post-Fordist consumption and consumer sovereignty actually exists is a matter of considerable debate. Keat (1991: 7) has argued that in order for consumers to possess any significant degree of sovereignty, consumer preferences would need to be generated 'independently of the plans and activities of producers'. Yet it appears the reverse is true, whereby producers have devoted even more resources to shaping and controlling the choices of consumers through the use of marketing and advertising. Glennie and Thrift (1992: 439) have also questioned whether the so-called 'new' forms of consumption are actually new. They have argued that 'preindustrial and postmodern forms of consumption have rather more in common than is acknowledged in much of the literature'. While Sivanandan (1989) has argued that for an increasing number of Britain's disinfranchised poor, post-Fordist consumption has little meaning.

The aim of this book is to explore some of the debates centring on consumer–producer relations as they have applied to the financial services sector in Britain in the 1980s and 1990s. The extent to which financial service organisations have become more consumer orientated will be evaluated, as will the view that power relations between producers and consumers have altered. The theme of Chapter 2 is to consider the reasons for the increase in the consumption of financial services in the 1980s and 1990s. Few attempts have been made to explore this issue, and most have linked the rise in financial service consumption to the level of income and wealth of individual consumers. It will be argued that such assessments are too simplistic, and that a range of complex social, economic and political processes need to be examined. The economic shift from manufacturing to service industries has been of considerable benefit in enabling financial service organisations to reach non-traditional, or under-represented consumers, such as women and manual workers. A number of demographic trends have also led to the increase in financial services. One important tendency is for the proportion of older people in the population of advanced industrial societies such as Britain to expand. 'Gold among the grey' is an apt description of a group in the population who are increasingly seeking out financial packages to suit their needs. Another group of consumers who have become active users of financial institutions in recent years are young people. While the demographic 'time bomb' has meant that there will be fewer numbers of young people, they are increasingly becoming more financially aware at an earlier age. Finally, government policy has also been influential in generating a demand for particular financial service products. The 'right to buy' policy of selling council housing at discount prices fuelled the demand for mortgages. The privatisation of public utilities generated the demand for shares and a share dealing expertise within financial service organisations. The Social Security Act 1986 also gave employees the option of investing in private pension plans, which increased the demand for investment advice and products.

The activities of producers in contributing to the expansion of financial services is the focus of Chapter 3. Financial service producers have gone to considerable lengths both to retain existing and to attract new consumers. The re-designing of financial service premises to promote a more user-friendly image was the most visible sign of this transition. The proliferation of new financial service products was another important trend. No longer were all-purpose accounts and policies targeted at the mass market, but segmented according to a range of variables including: lifestyle; age; stage in the life cycle; gender; socio-economic group; and home-ownership. The use of branding and the significant expenditure devoted to advertising are also indicative of this new-found marketing focus. Throughout the 1980s the financial service sector was the largest spender on advertising, ahead of the traditional high spending categories of food and motor cars. However, despite this massive injection of funds, financial service producers were at a disadvantage compared with their manufacturing counterparts. The extensive product development in which financial services organisations engaged during the 1980 and 1990s meant they could spend a proportionately small amount of their advertising budgets on promoting individual brands. This feature posed particular problems for banks who promote around 300 services, a much higher number than building societies and insurance companies. Many accounts of strategic marketing present it as an unproblematic activity. However, this emphasis underestimates the difficulties which can occur, and the risks which producers have to attempt to minimise. In this chapter, marketing strategies adopted by financial institutions will be outlined and critically evaluated. Where appropriate, examples from a case study at Northbank (a British clearing bank) will be used (see Appendix).

Faced with high levels of price and product competition, one of the ways in which financial institutions have attempted to gain competitive advantage has been through the promotion of service quality. This image was projected by company slogans, 'You get a little Xtra help at the Halifax', 'You're Better off talking to Barclays', 'T yeS B' all aimed at trying to win over the customer's confidence. In Chapter 4 an evaluation of some of the changes financial service organisations have made to their human resource policies to promote a more consumer-orientated focus will be assessed. There has evidently been a shift from organisational cultures which were conservative, reactive and cautious, and where the main element of the job was administration. Contemporary financial service personnel are required to be proactive, entrepreneurial and possess a high level of interpersonal skills and marketing expertise. To reinforce this orientation, a range of new employment practices has been developed. Training systems, customer care policies, quality circles and performance related pay schemes have been introduced by financial institutions to manage change and heighten the profile of the consumer among staff. However, despite the considerable resources invested in human resource management initiatives, it is not at all clear that some of these schemes have actually worked. Some of the problems financial institutions have confronted along this path will be considered using a case study of Northbank.

Chapters 3 and 4 considered attempts by producers to manipulate consumer demand for their particular services. In Chapter 5 the ways in which consumers have used financial services in a manner which was not intended or expected by producers will be examined. One recent trend has been for consumers to change financial service provider on a more frequent basis. This particularly applies to younger people and consumers from the higher socio-economic categories. Another flourishing practice has been dual account holding, whereby consumers hold accounts at more than one financial institution. The move towards the integrated financial supermarket which provides a variety of financial service products under one roof seems to be at odds with how some consumers actually behave in practice. Despite extensive advertising to promote automated payments such as direct debits, the take up rate has remained low and has met with considerable consumer resistance. In the 1980s, large numbers of consumers began to use their credit cards as a way of accessing an interest free overdraft, by paying their account in full at the end of the month, rather than to access credit and pay interest. These and other examples will be used to illustrate the inability of producers to manipulate consumers to a point where their behaviour becomes predictable. Consumers make active choices for themselves about which services to use, and which to discard. Some of the more educated consumers are increasingly learning how to play the system to their benefit.

The discussion in the previous chapters centres on the activities of producers and consumers, and the ways in which they have interacted with each other in the 1980s and 1990s. However, it would be somewhat simplistic to assess the consumer–producer relationship without making reference to the social context in which this interaction has occurred. Particularly influential in the 1980s was the role of government legislation. The Conservative government under Thatcher actively promoted the philosophy of competition and consumer choice. The aim of the 1986 Financial Services Act was to protect individual consumers against unscrupulous producers. A host of self-regulatory bodies were set up to regulate the industry and protect consumers. Similarly, the period 1981–91 was the decade when all four of the Financial Service Ombudsmen schemes were established. Ombudsmen schemes presented consumers with a systematic route to complain about financial service organisations on a free-of-charge basis. The growing number of consumer complaints being dealt with by the Ombudsmen has indicated that a greater number of consumers are actively promoting their own interests.

Consumerism in the financial services sector was undoubtedly a product of the 1980s. The National Consumer Council conducted several influential research reports relating to the financial services industry from the consumers' viewpoint. The Consumers' Association also continues publishing the results of its investigations of financial services through its *Which?* magazine. Every daily newspaper currently has a column offering advice and guidance on money matters, and the net effect has been that the mass media has critically assessed both financial service institutions and their products in the public sphere. The Monopolies and Mergers Commission and the Office of Fair Trading have regularly been at the centre of debates relating to the 'consumer interest' in the 1980s and 1990s. The contribution of legislation, Financial Services Ombudsmen and consumer groups in supporting the consumer's point of view will be discussed in Chapter 6.

In Chapter 7 the view that the power relations between producers and consumers has fundamentally changed will be critically evaluated. There are still a relatively small number of financial service providers from which consumers can purchase financial services. This situation is particularly relevant to banks. Many financial institutions have also engaged in substantial cost-cutting programmes, and reduced the numbers of branches and staff. Both of these strategies cannot be in the consumers' best interest, yet consumers and consumer groups are powerless to resist such changes. The widespread use of information technology has also encouraged that standardisation of credit referencing and credit scoring procedures. It will be argued that this practice gives producers a considerable degree of power over consumers.

This chapter also considers the likely effects of the Single European Market (SEM) for financial service consumers. The SEM has been presented as a considerable benefit for consumers. However, an examination of the SEM in financial services suggests that the projected benefits for consumers have been overestimated. Given the moves towards increasing the availability of financial service redress procedures available to consumers in Britain, it is disappointing to note that consumer protection has not been given a high priority by the European Commission. Rather than services being expanded, because of the likely event that cross-border trade may increase the number and complexity of consumer complaints and difficulties, services have been cut. There is no integrated pan-European system for assessing complaints against financial service firms, as there is in Britain through the Ombudsmen schemes. Many European countries are also less well served by consumer groups promoting the interests of consumers than Britain. The chapter concludes by acknowledging that while financial service institutions have become more consumer-orientated, the power within the relationship still lies firmly in the hands of producers.

# Chapter 2

# The emergence of the financial service consumer

Since the mid-1970s, the expansion in the numbers of financial service consumers in Britain has been remarkable. By 1991, 92 per cent of the adult population had a financial service account. The percentage of the population holding a building society account doubled over the period, from 30–60 per cent (see Table 2.1). Fewer than 4 million adults in Britain have no bank or building society account. Non-account holders tend to be confined to a narrow range of social groups, including unskilled employees; individuals living on state benefit in the lowest socio-economic groups and people who are not economically active such as housewives and young people in the 16–24 age category (Association of Payment Clearing Services 1992). The purchase of life assurance tends to be lower than for account holding. Around 50 per cent of the population have some form of life assurance, although the figure for men is higher than for women (Watkins 1990).

While there has clearly been an expansion in the consumption of financial services in recent years, there have been few attempts to assess why the increase has occurred. One explanation by Vittas and Frazer (1982) links the consumption of financial services to the level of income

Table 2.1 Trends in account holding in Britain, 1976–91

|  | 1976 | 1981 | % of adults<br>1984 | 1988 | 1991 |
|---|---|---|---|---|---|
| Any current account | 45 | 61 | 65 | 73 | 77 |
| Building society accounts | 30 | 50 | 51 | 61 | 60* |
| Any account | 68 | 85 | 87 | 88 | 92 |

Source: Association of Payment Clearing Services (1992).
Note: * Abbey National excluded since transfer to bank status.

and wealth of individual consumers. They have claimed that all individuals, irrespective of what society they live in, have three basic financial needs: the facility to save and borrow; the ability to make payments; and to be able to insure against financial loss. They suggest that individuals living in poor, underdeveloped countries cannot afford to save for future needs or borrow to meet current needs at the expense of future consumption. Within such societies the mode of exchange is often bartering, and the demand from consumers for a specialised payment system is either minimal or non-existent. Likewise, people who have no regular income from employment, or little material wealth, are hardly likely to be predisposed towards insuring against financial loss. However, Vittas and Frazer conclude that these factors do not necessarily indicate that individuals living in less advanced economies do not have the three basic financial needs, but that their weak economic position inhibits them from expressing the desire for superior financial arrangements.

Vittas and Frazer's (1982) conceptual analysis has a number of practical outcomes. As societies become more affluent, consumers' financial needs become more sophisticated, and they require increasingly specialised services. A growing premium is placed on time, and services such as Automatic Teller Machines (ATMs) are introduced to provide a more convenient service. A greater degree of geographical mobility necessitates the need for payment facilities which are widely accepted. Because of the increased affluence of the population, saving out of existing income becomes a possibility and reality for the majority. This factor generates demand for investment and advice services. Finally, the possibility and likelihood of career advancement, and improved financial security, reduces the barriers to borrowing and gives rise to the demand for consumer credit.

There are a number of factors which support Vittas and Frazer's (1982) view that the level of income and wealth of consumers determines the level of financial services consumption within a particular society. For example, some of the more underdeveloped countries in the world have relatively unsophisticated financial service provision when contrasted with an advanced economy such as Britain's. It also tends to be the more affluent sections of society that are extensive consumers of financial services. Often the availability of financial services is dependent on individual or household income. Time saving delivery mechanisms have also been introduced, such as increasingly sophisticated ATMs which provide self service statements, inter account transfers, and bill payments. New ways of delivering services, such as telephone banking (First Direct) and buying insurance over the telephone (Direct Line), have led to the consumption of financial services becoming spatially indifferent (Burton 1990). However, despite its merits, problems arise with their explanation because they present a rather simple, causal relationship between income and wealth, and the consumption of financial services. While they acknowledge that there are substantial variations in the use of financial services between people of different ages, gender, and social class, which reflect wider cultural, religious, and socio-psychological attitudes, their conceptualisation of these additional variables is underdeveloped.

In this chapter it will be demonstrated that the consumption of financial services in Britain is the result of a number of highly complex social, economic and political processes. A number of themes will be developed to substantiate this viewpoint. The first will relate to shifts in the composition of the workforce within the British economy in the last twenty years. The trend towards the service economy has provided more opportunities for women to work, and has opened up the possibility that they may become more active consumers of financial services. The shift from a predominantly manual to a non-manual workforce in Britain has also indirectly led to an increase in the consumption of financial services. A second area of discussion relates to recent demographic changes which have had a positive effect on financial service consumption, both in relation to older and younger citizens. A third theme will relate to the changing consumer attitudes towards credit and debt. Finally, the role of government policies in promoting the use of financial services will be discussed.

## WOMEN, WORK AND FINANCIAL SERVICES

The number of women in the labour force has increased substantially in most Western societies since the 1960s, and Britain is no exception in this regard. Women currently represent nearly 50 per cent of the workforce. The expansion of employment opportunities for women is partly a consequence of shifts within industries and occupations in the British economy. An important trend in recent years has been a growth in service sector industries and occupations such as banking and finance, tourism, and personal services (Graham *et al.* 1989). There has been a corresponding decline in predominantly male, manufacturing employment. Because of the gender stereotyping of many service occupations as women's work, these industrial shifts have increased employment opportunities for women. Other important contributory factors have been the large-scale availability of part-time work, and the fact that it has become more acceptable for women to work after childbirth.

It has been apparent for some time that women are much more likely to have a bank account if they are engaged in paid work. This trend is observable whether or not women work on a full- or part-time basis (York and Hayes 1982). The movement towards working women being more extensive users of financial services than women undertaking unpaid work in the home is a characteristic which is not confined to Britain. Bartos's (1989) study of women in ten countries across four continents concluded that career women were the most financially active segment among women in every society. The opposite was true for housewives, who were less likely to have a financial service account. The trend for women to become more extensive users of financial services is reflected in the statistics for current account holding. In Britain, it has historically been the case that fewer women than men possessed a current account, but by the mid-1980s this gap had been virtually eliminated (Equal Opportunities Commission 1989).

Financial institutions have been slow to acknowledge the importance of women as financial service consumers. This began to change in the 1980s, when accounts, advertising, dedicated leaflets and financial service guides were targeted at women. However, despite the increasing numbers of women who are consumers of financial services, the treatment they have received at the hands of financial institutions has often left a lot to be desired. The Sex Discrimination Act 1975 made it unlawful for financial institutions to discriminate on the grounds of sex. However, despite legislation to prevent discrimination, the Equal Opportunities Commission (EOC) has received a number of complaints by women. These have included issues such as,

> refusal of loans; insistence on male guarantors; full-time employment requirements; men being the first named on joint accounts and mortgages (with important practical consequences); additional requirements being placed on women seeking to raise start-up capital for small businesses; inexplicably lower credit card limits than for comparable men; and complaints that financial institutions seemed to treat women less favourably than their male counterparts.
>
> (EOC 1989: Preface)

In an attempt to eliminate sex bias from credit scoring systems, the EOC has published a number of guides such as *Sex Equality and Credit-Scoring* (1986), and *Credit for Women* (1988). The EOC has also attempted to raise women's awareness of the importance of pensions in its publication *Your Pension Matters* (1992). The EOC (1989b) has even provided training exercises for bank customer contact staff and trainees in an attempt to eliminate discrimination across the bank counter.

Women have already become important consumers of financial services in their own right, and will continue to be so in the future. An additional reason for the expansion of financial services, which is also employment related, is the repeal of the Truck Acts. The next section charts the key features of the Act which has generated an increase in the use of financial services among manual workers.

## A SHIFT FROM MANUAL TO NON-MANUAL WORKERS: SOME IMPLICATIONS OF THE REPEAL OF THE TRUCK ACTS

The repeal of the Truck Acts, which came into effect on 1 January 1987, gave financial institutions an enormous opportunity to increase their numbers of consumers. Since 1464 statutes had been used to restrict the abuses of the Truck System, whereby workers were paid with credits which had to be spent in shops under the ownership or control of their employer. The Truck Acts safeguarded employees from exploitative employers by stating that manual employees had to be paid in 'the coin of the realm'. The effect of the Truck Acts on the method of payment of manual workers in Britain was extensive. In the early 1980s the proportion of the workforce paid in cash and on a weekly basis in Britain was much higher than many other advanced, industrial societies. The percentage in Britain was around 50 per cent, compared with 15 per cent in Holland, 5 per cent in France, Germany, and Canada, and a mere 1 per cent in the USA (Lewis 1982; OECD 1989). After the Truck Acts were repealed, employers were no longer under the statutory obligation to pay manual workers in cash. Furthermore, once cashless pay had been chosen by employees, their decision was irrevocable. The position of non-manual workers has remained unchanged throughout, as they were not covered by the original Truck Acts.

The repeal of the Truck Acts has been particularly important in generating more financial service users among manual employees. Prior to the repeal of the Act there was little necessity on the part of weekly paid, blue collar workers to hold a bank or building society current account, unless they chose to. However, by 1992 almost two-thirds of working people had their salary paid directly into a bank or building society account. This was in contrast to a mere 20 per cent of employees who were paid cash (Association of Payment Clearing Services 1992). The observable shift from weekly to fortnightly or even monthly pay has also proved important in generating business for the banks and building societies, given that around 80 per cent of monthly salaries are automated (APACS 1988).

An extensive study into the the adoption of cashless pay (Industrial Relations Review and Report 1990) found there were major advantages to be gained by employers. The primary benefit was the reduction in administrative costs, especially if the move to cashless pay was associated with a switch from weekly to fortnightly or monthly pay. Significant reductions in security costs were also cited as an important feature of cashless pay. The main disadvantage stemmed from employers having to operate two systems when the majority of employees had converted but there was a hard core who refused to do so.

The banks have been active supporters of cashless pay, for the obvious reasons of attracting accounts, and thereby opening up the possibility of cross-selling various bank services. In 1987 the Committee of London and Scottish Bankers (CLSB), the industry's information service, published an employers' guide to the repeal of the Truck Acts. Individual banks have also provided staff to give presentations, and have provided information packs to workplaces in an attempt to highlight the convenience and ease of opening a bank account. On occasions cash points, or other means of employees being able to access their account, have been offered in remote sites.

Shifts within the labour market in Britain have had a positive effect on the consumption of financial services in the last twenty years. In the next section, the increase in the consumption of financial services will be considered in the context of the changing demographic profile observable in Britain.

## GOLD AMONG THE GREY: FINANCIAL SERVICES AND THE OLDER CONSUMER

Approximately one in five of the population in most European countries will be over 65 years of age by the beginning of the next century. In the decade 1990 to 2000, there will be a 20 per cent increase in the population who are in their fifties in Britain (Johnson 1990). Because of this huge expansion, the older segment of the population will provide continuing opportunities for financial service providers. The image presented of the over fifty-fives is often rather downbeat, and dominated by that of poor pensioners who are dependent on welfare and charity. However, this impression bears little resemblance to reality. Since the 1970s the proportion of pensioners in Europe living in poverty has declined, while the proportion of families with children living in poverty has increased (Johnson 1990). Within Britain, individuals over 55 years of age are the richest segment of the population. They are a particularly important source of savings for the building societies and national savings (Buck 1990).

Johnson (1990) has suggested that the accumulation of wealth among the 'grey' has a variety of sources. First, the coverage of occupational pensions has never been greater. This feature, combined with the greater value of pensions, has meant that larger sections of the older population are wealthier than previous generations. Second, older citizens benefited from relatively high interest rates during the 1980s, and capital gains in the equities market on their savings. Third, in most instances the capital gains resulting from home-ownership have been considerable in recent years. The longer individuals have owned their property the more extensive the capital gains accumulated is likely to be (Saunders 1990). Almost all owner-occupiers over the age of 65 own their property outright. Similarly, in the age category 50–65, over half the population own their own homes. A final factor which has contributed to the increased wealth of the over fifties age group is that the average age of inheritance is currently 55. At this age, individuals have usually paid off their mortgage and their children have 'flown the nest'. Not surprisingly, the financial services which older people predominantly use are savings based. They use few credit facilities such as loans, credit cards and hire purchase. Older people are significant users of financial services and this has contributed to the overall increase in the use of financial services in Britain. They are also frequently loyal to financial service organisations, and are good prospects for cross-selling. They also tend to limit the financial services companies they deal with because of convenience (Doyle and Seekamp 1989). However, because of the images which are often portrayed of older people, they have been relatively 'invisible' consumers. In his research in the late 1980s, Banks (1990) found that older sections of the population felt ignored and patronised by financial service organisations. Few financial service institutions provided services specifically for the over 55 age group. Although the results of the survey did indicate that building societies were more sensitive than either banks or insurance companies.

Another growth area in financial services since the 1980s, and one which has been given a high profile, is the expansion of accounts aimed at young people.

## THE GROWTH IN ACCOUNTS FOR YOUNGER PEOPLE

New consumers to financial services in recent years have been younger people, whether they be school children, students or young people starting their first job. To a large extent, financial service accounts have begun to replace the piggy bank. A range of providers including friendly societies, unit and investment trusts, national savings, banks and building societies have all promoted savings facilities for children. Some of these have catchy names such as Children's Bonus Bonds and Halifax's Little Extra Club. The demographic decline in the form of a 20 per cent reduction in the 15–19-year-old population by 1992 has made attracting this group of consumers a high priority for financial service organisations. The 15–24-year-old category have considerable discretionary purchasing power in their own right. In 1979 they received an estimated £540 million in pocket money (Irvine 1980). This is a figure which must have increased considerably, and does not include gifts and earned income (Lewis 1982). However, the main reason why financial institutions have wanted to attract young consumers is because of the possibility that young people will keep their account at the same institution as adults. Yorkshire Bank has been at the forefront of pioneering school accounts and this effort appears to have paid good dividends. The bank estimates that over 300,000 of their 1.3 million current account holders had contact with the bank as children (Thomson 1992b). Midland Bank has also estimated that around 75 per cent of children who held accounts with the bank remain with them throughout their banking life (Doyle and Seekamp 1989).

A novel approach pioneered by Midland Bank to attract young consumers in the mid-1980s was its Mid-Bank scheme. Mid-Bank is operated by pupils of schools who run their own bank and offer school children a range of services. The scheme operates in approximately 1,500 schools throughout the country and is particularly popular in affluent, middle-class areas. The scheme provides an opportunity for Midland to attract young consumers, recruit future staff, and provide a subject of enquiry for business studies students. However, not all financial institutions have accepted the view that catching consumers young is a useful strategy. The Leeds Permanent Building Society relinquished 500 of its school branches to Yorkshire Bank. The Leeds were of the opinion that consumers choose different financial service institutions for a variety of reasons, none of which were related to whether they had an account as a child (Thomson 1992b).

Student accounts have another function besides attracting new consumers. They have often provided a market research function for testing out adult accounts. For example, Lloyds was the first of the four major British banks to offer interest bearing current accounts, which it initially tested on the youth market. Headway offered interest on deposits and provided a cheque book to savers over 15 years of age. In the first six months after it was launched, Headway was reputed to have signed up to 30,000 customers. This positive response encouraged the launch of Classic, an interest bearing current account for adults, as a response to competitive pressures from the building societies who had entered the current account market for the first time.

Both changes in the demographic profile and the composition of the workforce have been important contributory factors in the expansion of financial services in Britain in recent years. A more recent phenomenon, the increase in credit and debt, has to be situated within the context of changing consumer attitudes. Some of the reasons to account for changing perceptions of credit and debt are considered more closely in the next section.

## CONSUMER CREDIT AND DEBT

The most extraordinary expansion of financial service business, and one which has probably caused the most concern, is the expansion of consumer credit and debt. The increase is demonstrated by the fact that during the mid-1980s, banks were in the astonishing position of lending more to personal sector borrowers than industry (British Bankers Association 1993). The extensive acceptance of credit by consumers has been particularly advantageous for financial service providers. Consumer finance is also relatively price insensitive, which has meant profitable consumer loans have often subsidised unprofitable areas of business. The growth in the number of credit cards issued, and the amount borrowed, whether it be from financial institutions or retailers, has been extensive. A recent Policy Studies survey (see Berthoud and Kempson 1992) indicated that four out of ten households possessed a credit card. However, the study revealed that credit cards were not the most common source of credit. Despite their working-class image, mail order catalogues were the most extensively used form of credit and they were used to a similar extent across all, except the very highest, social groups.

The availability of credit is not new – it has always been available – however, the form it has taken has changed over time (Parker 1990). Most of the borrowing and lending prior to the Industrial Revolution took place between borrowers and lenders who were personally known to each other. There was also a distinction between the type of credit available to different social groups. While the gentry 'ran up bills', the pauper 'pawned her wedding ring' (National Consumer Council 1990: 25). More recently, this relationship has been transformed, and is now characterised by a series of continuous, regular and organised transactions between credit providers and individuals (Ford 1988).

Why the expansion of consumer credit occurred in the 1980s is debatable. One reason might be that obtaining credit became much easier. This was especially the case after 1982, when the Conservative government removed all existing credit controls. Prior to 1982 consumers were required to save up a deposit for goods to be bought on credit. This was usually a quarter of the purchase price in the case of white goods, and one-third of the price of a motor vehicle. After credit controls were lifted, consumers were able to obtain loans which represented 100 per cent of the purchase price of goods and services. This feature, combined with the promotion of interest free credit by manufacturers and retailers, has been a considerable inducement for people to borrow.

There has also been an increase in the number of sources from which consumers can purchase credit. Ford (1991) has identified four categories of lender. The first are commercial, legally regulated market transactions by financial institutions such as bank loans, or store cards. The second group consists of informal, non-market based loans from friends or family. The third category includes government loans. Since 1988 government policy has shifted from providing financial support in the form of grants, to credit agreements. The social fund loan system is an example of this change in state policy. The final category identified are unregulated, extortionate market transactions, such as those associated with money lenders and loan sharks.

While Ford (1991) provides a useful fourfold categorisation, she omits another expanding source of credit. Community-based credit unions are financial service providers, yet their role has often been neglected. The most extensive study on the topic was undertaken by Berthoud and Hinton (1989) on behalf of the Policy Studies Institute. The first credit union in Britain was formed in 1964 in a London suburb. By 1980, fifty-seven unions existed, and their numbers increased dramatically throughout the 1980s. In 1988, 142 credit unions were registered in Britain with a total membership of approximately 35,000. The study revealed that credit union members were comprised of individuals from most occupational categories. Nevertheless, the unemployed and women were disproportionately represented among credit union members. This final point highlights the financial responsibility which women undertake within households.

It is highly likely that the variety of sources of credit available to consumers in the 1980s may have had an impact on its expansion. However, it needs to be acknowledged that an increase in the number of credit providers does not necessarily result in an automatic increase in uptake of facilities. A precondition of the growth of consumer credit has been consumer acceptability. As Fortescue has illustrated:

> Things have altered since the perhaps apocryphal North Country British housewife refused to use the washing machine bought by her husband on hire purchase until the last payment was made. The attitude is now closer to the American one. I'd rather drive a car that's not paid for, than save up for a car that my wife's next husband will have the pleasure of driving.
>
> (Fortescue 1987: 127)

A similar point has been made by Lewis (1982: 43) when she states 'Attitudes towards, and motivations for, borrowing have changed a great deal. Borrowing is no longer considered to be shameful, an admission of weakness, and evidence of a lack of restraint'. One of the main reasons Lewis cites for the increase in credit is that consumers feel more financially secure because of state intervention in the form of unemployment benefit, pensions and other financial help. A similar explanation, but from a financial service provider's perspective, has been advanced by Russell (1975). He has argued that high levels of employment, made possible through government intervention in monetary and fiscal policy, has enabled banks to trust consumers to repay their debts.

So far the discussion has focused upon consumer credit. However, most of the recent concern relates to the increase in consumer debt. While it could be argued that all forms of credit are also debt, most consumers have few problems in fulfilling their credit agreements. The distinction needs to be made between credit and debt, with debt indicating that people have commitments which cause financial problems by way of arrears and default. A National Consumer Council report in 1989 concluded that British families were the most indebted in Europe. They had 20 per cent more debt than their French and German counterparts, and three times more than the Italians and the Dutch. Britain also had substantially higher interest rates for borrowing than many other European countries. The top interest rates in Britain were nearly twenty times higher than those in other European countries. The number of households becoming so highly geared that they were unable to pay their debts also exhibited a large increase throughout the 1980s, up from 1.3 million in 1981 to 2 million by 1989.

A range of explanations has been suggested to account for the rise in consumer debt. Berthoud and Kempson (1992) have indicated that they fall into two main categories. On the one hand, there are those which are debtor focused, and include reasons such as poverty, changes in life circumstances, and the view that some people are unable to manage money. Alternative explanations are creditor focused, and give a higher profile to the activities of financial institutions. According to this line of reasoning, financial institutions are responsible for the growth in debt because they have encouraged overcommitment, have levied excess charges and have made inappropriate arrangements for collecting payments. In fact the process of obtaining credit has become little more than a formality, and is usually made as pleasant and seductive as possible. It has an 'anonymous' quality which enables the applicant to merely fill in an application form. As a result of the extensive introduction of credit scoring, the ordeal of an interview with a bank manager or other official has become redundant.

The rise in consumer credit and debt has been significant in Britain since the 1980s. However, consumer credit in the form of personal loans and credit card balances are the tip of the iceberg in relation to the total amount of credit extended by financial institutions. Credit cards and personal loans only account for around 15 per cent of personal sector lending. By far the biggest credit item for most people is their mortgage. In the next section, the expansion of mortgage finance will be assessed within the context of the recent increase in home-ownership.

## A PROPERTY-OWNING DEMOCRACY? THE GROWTH OF HOME-OWNERSHIP IN THE 1980s

Owner-occupation accounts for approximately 65 per cent of housing tenure in Britain. This compares with 43 per cent in West Germany, 85 per cent in Spain, and 51 per cent in France (Evans 1988; Holmes 1992). Home-ownership in Britain increased during the 1980s, both in relation to the proportion of people owning their own homes and in relation to the value of mortgage finance loaned to buyers. The reasons for the increase in owner-occupation is much debated. Respondents in Saunders' (1990) sample of home-owners in four localities in Britain in 1987 indicated a number of reasons why they had become owner-occupiers. However, the most frequently cited reasons were associated with the autonomy that home-ownership offered, and that property was considered an appreciating asset with the prospect of significant capital gains.

To some extent, recent rises in home-ownership can be explained by the privatisation of public housing. The 'right to buy' local authority housing, as a consequence of the Housing Act 1980, and the Tenant's Right (Scotland) Act 1980, gave the occupiers the option to buy providing they had held security of tenure for at least three years. Following the Housing and Building Control Act 1984, the qualifying period was reduced to two years. Between 1980 and 1982 the sale of local authority and New Town housing increased from 93,000 to 228,000 properties. During the remainder of the 1980s sales stabilised, but still remained high at an average of over 100,000 annually, compared with approximately 30,000 a year in the 1970s. Even in the recession-hit late 1980s, the 1989 General Household Survey revealed that 12 per cent of local authority tenants were actively considering buying their own home, a similar percentage to 1981 (Social Trends 1989; Breeze *et al.* 1991).

Both of the Housing Acts clearly structured the demand for mortgages. Indeed most of the rise in home-ownership since 1979 has been dependent on the availability of mortgage finance. During the decade 1979 to 1989, the proportion of households with a mortgage increased from 30–42 per cent, while the proportion of the population renting from local authorities declined from 34–24 per cent. However, it is not merely government policies which have discriminated in favour of home-ownership which have stimulated the growth in the mortgage market. Ironically, negative state policies have also had the same effect. A case in point was the five months' notice given in the 1988 Budget that multiple mortgage tax relief was to be abolished. Personal borrowing, for the most part mortgage finance, peaked in the third quarter of 1988 and has decelerated ever since (British Bankers' Association 1992).

The relatively profitable nature of mortgage lending acted as an incentive to financial service producers to enter the market in the 1980s. Rather than mortgage lending being the virtually exclusive domain of the building societies, insurance companies and banks began to aggressively market themselves as providers of mortgage finance. The 'packaging' and cross-selling of services for home-owners such as property and life insurance became apparent. As a consequence of the increased competition in the mortgage market, consumers were able to secure larger multiples of their salary, or loans representing a greater proportion of the purchase price of their home, than had previously been the case. In 1987, for example, 50 per cent of first time buyers obtained a mortgage of 95 per cent or more on the purchase price of their home (Bank of England Quarterly Bulletin 1989).

For many families and individuals, the dream of owning their own home turned sour. In the early 1990s mortgage arrears and household repossessions were running at record levels. In 1981, 5,000 homes were repossessed, and by 1991 this figure had increased to 36,500 (Social Trends 1992). Whether or not these trends will continue is debatable, and there are arguments both ways (Ford 1992). Similarly, lenders who considered mortgage finance as a profitable area of business have been left with unpaid loans. The government's attempts at 'kick-starting' the housing market, by announcing a 'holiday' on stamp duty for six months in the first half of 1992, had little impact on the growing housing crisis. The alternative policy, promoted by financial institutions, suggesting that losses sustained by home-owners should qualify for tax relief, fell on 'deaf' ears at the Treasury.

State policies in the 1980s which urged people to buy their own homes clearly helped to generate mortgages and credit for other consumer goods. Another area of government policy which has contributed to the increase in financial services was the privatisation programmes, which generated the demand for shares.

## PRIVATISATION AND SHARE OWNERSHIP

An important area of state policy which structured the demand for shares in the 1980s was the privatisation of various nationalised companies. The move towards privatisation and shareownership was the deliberate policy of the Conservative government. This sentiment was reflected in the Chancellor of the Exchequer's Budget Speech in 1986 when he stated, 'It is the long-term ambition of this government to make the British people a nation of shareowners; to create popular capitalism, in which more and more men and women have a direct personal stake in British business and Industry.' An incentive for people to buy was the underpricing of many of the share issues which offered the prospect of immediate capital gains. Extraordinary amounts of advertising were also devoted to promoting share flotations. The 'Tell Sid' campaign associated with the privatisation of British Gas illustrated this trend.

The increase in shareholding activity in the 1980s resulted in share ownership becoming more widely spread in Britain than in any other major industrial nation, except the USA (Lamont 1988). In 1987, the New York Stock Exchange estimated between 20–7 per cent of the adult population of the USA owned shares or unit trusts. The comparable figure for Britain was 21 per cent. Nevertheless, the British figure remained high in comparison to France, where in 1985 the figure was 9 per cent; and in Japan only 5 per cent of the population owned shares. In 1990 the Treasury estimated that 11 million people in Britain owned shares, approximately 24 per cent of the population (HM Treasury 1987, 1989).

Notable privatisations have included the sale of British Telecom in November 1984, the sale of British Gas in December 1986 and 31.5 per cent of BP in October 1987. On a much smaller scale there has been the relatively new method of employee buy-outs of public companies such as National Freight and Vickers in March 1986 (Standen 1988). Of the 13 per cent of adults who held shares in privatised companies, more than half had never owned shares before. However, two-fifths of all shareholders only held shares in privatised companies, or the Trustee Savings Bank. Privatisation has clearly been the major factor behind the increase in share ownership since 1979.

What the figures relating to share ownership do not include, however, are the number of times that shares were bought and then sold. Nor do they indicate the commissions made by financial services intermediaries undertaking the buying and selling of shares on behalf of their clients. The turnover of buying and selling shares in privatised companies was enormous. For example, 3 million people held shares in British Airways after it had been privatised in 1987. Three months later this figure had declined to 420,000. Likewise, 2.3 million people held shares in British Telecom upon privatisation; two and a half years later BT had only 1.4 million shareholders (Vickers and Yarrow 1988). The commissions associated with selling shares were a source of risk-free revenue for financial institutions during a period of declining profitability. One result of the increased demand for buying and selling shares was the introduction of share shops within high street branches. The buying and selling of shares was transformed from an activity confined to the intimacy of the bank manager's office, to a public sphere activity with interactive screens and 'on-the-spot share dealing'. Touchscreen instant share dealing is available at 270 NatWest branches alone.

Another area of government privatisation which received little extensive attention was the promotion of personal, as opposed to state, pension plans. In 1986 the government passed the Social Security Act which enabled employees to opt out of State Earnings-Related Pension Schemes (SERPS) and buy their own pensions. This policy was presented as an important benefit for consumers as it gave them the flexibility to keep the same pension when they changed job. The Act also presented a considerable opportunity for financial service firms to promote a high value added area of business. After the Act took effect in April 1988, the Prudential exhibited a 25 per cent increase in its number of private pension plan sales (Retail Banker International 1989). Many financial service organisations in Britain have viewed high value added products as one of the most profitable ways forward in the 1990s. This is because for many other financial services, especially those involved with money transmission, Britain is considered a 'mature' marketplace (Gavaghan 1990).

## CONCLUSION

While Vittas and Frazer's (1982) explanation of the demand for financial services as being dependent on the income and wealth of individual consumers was a useful starting point, it suffered from being too economically deterministic. Their explanation emphasises economic factors at the expense of important social, demographic and political processes. The notion of an evolutionary trajectory underestimates the effect of intervention, whether that be in the form of the state, or from the consumers themselves. In the case of Britain, the social construction of housing and other forms of consumption as indicators of social status and success have fuelled the expansion of consumer credit. Changes in the composition of the workforce have also contributed to the increase in financial services, as have government privatisation programmes. However, the actions of financial service institutions have also been influential in determining the consumption of financial services in Britain. Financial organisations have not been passive bystanders, mere spectators, in the last ten years. On the contrary, they have gone to great lengths to aggressively market themselves to consumers. The next chapter considers some of the strategies which financial institutions have adopted to attract and keep consumers.

## SUMMARY

A number of factors have led to the expansion in the numbers of financial services consumers in Britain. They have included:

1  an increase in the numbers of women in the workforce;
2  the repeal of the Truck Acts;
3  demographic trends;
4  changing consumer attitudes towards credit;
5  government privatisation polices.

# Chapter 3

# Financial services go to market

In the previous chapter, a number of factors were identified as giving rise to the increase in financial service consumption in the 1980s and 1990s. This chapter will focus on the strategies employed by financial service producers to generate a demand for financial services. There has been a great deal of recent discussion about the relationship between producers and consumers. One view is that producers, in this case financial service firms, have manipulated consumers to purchase their services through the use of sophisticated marketing techniques and advertising. It could be argued that deregulation has placed increased emphasis on producers to engage in product diversification, product differentiation, and to search out market niches. According to this interpretation of events, the increased consumption of financial services in recent years has been a result of strategies employed by financial service firms to heighten consumer demand.

This view of the relationship between producers and consumers is not universally shared. According to Campbell (1987), scenarios which have depicted producers manipulating consumers for their own ends are too simplistic. He notes that consumers have at their disposal a range of cultural influences upon which they can draw to 'decode' advertising messages independently of producers. Consumers are therefore able to draw on their own life experiences, and that of others, to critically evaluate marketing material presented by producers. He also believes that the market for goods and services is not homogeneous. Therefore, different individual consumers will react to advertising messages in different ways. While producers can control the delivery of advertisements in the press and on television, they cannot predict how they will be received and understood by consumers. Finally, Campbell doubts that consumers unilaterally accept what they are told by producers in an uncritical way. The view that consumers passively accept what they are told in the ads is somewhat naive.

The consumer–producer relationship has also been discussed by Urry (1990). He argues that there have been a number of distinctive changes between consumers and producers in the last twenty years. He conceptualises the changing nature of the relationship as a shift from mass to post-Fordist consumption. Mass consumption is characterised by the 'pile it high and sell it cheap strategy' of the major supermarkets which emerged in the 1960s. During the era of mass consumption, producers, rather than consumers, were most influential as individual firms dominated particular industrial markets. Market segmentation was in its infancy, and mass-produced products did not significantly vary according to the requirements of different consumer markets. Post-Fordist consumption differs from mass consumption in several fundamental ways. There is increased competition between producers as a result of deregulation which prompts producers to segment the mass market in order to service consumer needs more effectively. A higher profile is given to product development, and segmentation variables become more diverse. In particular, there are many more products which have a shorter life cycle, and there is a growing trend towards the 'politicising' and 'greening' of consumption. The consumer, rather than the producer becomes dominant. The growth of consumer movements acting on behalf of consumers serves to reinforce this change in emphasis. Urry's message is that in an era of post-Fordist consumption, unless producers take account of the needs of consumers, they will become uncompetitive in an increasingly competitive marketplace.

Abercrombie (1991) has also considered the producer-consumer relationship. However, he has paid particular attention to the power relations between producers and consumers. Abercrombie argues that the reasons why firms have become more consumer orientated is not a consequence of producers manipulating or creating the conditions for new forms of consumption. Instead, he suggests that 'enterprising' consumers through their actions are forcing firms to change. As he states, 'Producers have lost, or are losing, much of their social position. In some senses, this is a loss of authority. It is loss of authority as producer in determining the form and content of production and consumption' (Abercrombie 1991: 172–3). A similar perspective has been propagated by a number of other writers. Gardener and Sheppard (1989: 50) believe consumers are key agents in the consumption process and they 'always get what they want through aggregate consumer choice'. Campbell (1987) goes further, and has suggested that consumer aspirations run ahead of the producers' ability to satisfy them. Therefore, the ability to meet the demands of 'sovereign' consumers has become the new and overriding institutional imperative. However, some commentators have argued that the predominant focus upon the 'enterprising' and 'sovereign' consumer has gone too far, because it underestimates the massive resources available to large firms and the power they wield (Keat 1991; Gardener and Sheppard 1989).

The aim of this chapter is to examine the ways in which financial service firms have attempted to manipulate consumer demand for their products. It will be argued that the process is rarely as straightforward as the manipulation theorists would have us believe. The chapter will focus on a number of pertinent issues, some of which are highlighted by a case study of Northbank, a British clearing bank (see Appendix). The first issue to be addressed is the evolution of the marketing function within financial service organisations. A precondition of firms being able to manipulate consumer demand is that they have in place an advanced and well-financed marketing function. A second issue to be examined is the extent and nature of financial service advertising. Financial firms were the largest spending advertising category throughout the 1980s. Despite the considerable financial resources earmarked for advertising, financial service firms have had to confront many difficult issues associated with promoting services as opposed to products. A third area of investigation will centre upon the nature of product innovation in the financial services industry, with particular emphasis upon the various segmentation strategies employed. Finally, the physical space in which the service delivery is undertaken has become an important area of concern in the financial services industry. The efforts made by financial service organisations to promote their premises as being more user friendly, and some of the problems they have encountered in doing so, will be highlighted.

## THE DEVELOPMENT OF MARKETING IN FINANCIAL INSTITUTIONS

Until the first signs of competition began to be felt in the mid-1970s, marketing was not perceived as a high profile activity by financial institutions. When financial sectors were constructed as separate entities, and regulation was used to keep competition to a minimum, there was little need or incentive for financial institutions to sustain a high marketing profile. However, deregulation has prompted financial service firms to engage in both price and product competition. An environment has been constructed whereby producers have to actively market themselves to consumers in an attempt to keep existing and generate new business. Several rounds of deregulation have been the dominant driving force behind the relatively recent marketing focus of many financial institutions (van der Merwe 1987).

Newman (1984) has indicated that it was not until the 1970s that building societies began to actively develop marketing strategies. The Woolwich established its marketing department in 1973, a similar point in time to the Provincial. The Halifax and the Abbey National set up theirs at the end of the 1970s. The arrival of marketing to banking, in a similar way to the building societies, has occurred fairly recently. Clarke *et al.* (1988) have employed a fourfold periodisation to identify distinctive periods in the evolution of bank marketing. The first stage, the 'production era', existed until the 1960s. This was a period when an inward focus predominated and the emphasis was on producing and selling. The next stage, the 'promotion era', occurred from the early 1960s and lasted until the early 1970s. At this point, the banks had begun to feel the limited effects of competition from the building societies. One response was to advertise service quality much more than had previously been the case. The banks entered the third stage, 'the marketing-orientated era', sometime during the early 1970s. The selling focus became prominent as more effort was directed at promotion. The final periodization, 'marketing control', represented a further intensification of the marketing orientation. It signalled the move to integrate marketing as the ultimate driving force within the whole organisation.

While Clarke *et al.* (1988) have provided a useful starting point in analysing the evolution of bank marketing, they have neglected to consider why the marketing focus developed more slowly in banking than in other areas of retailing. Watson (1982) has cited a number of reasons to account for this apparently slow development in banking, which are also applicable to other financial service industries. One important reason was the lack of marketing theory which was specifically directed towards the marketing of services, as opposed to manufactured goods. One of the earliest attempts to establish service marketing in its own right was Rathmell's book, *Marketing in the Service Sector*, published in 1974. This difficulty was overcome by the mid-1980s when service marketing management had become an integrated part of the marketing literature. A second difficulty related to the lack of a body of literature which specifically dealt with the marketing of banks and other financial services. The breakthrough in this area occurred with the publication of *Marketing Financial Services* (McIver and Naylor 1980). The third constraint identified by Watson was the change in organisational culture which was required to drive the new marketing focus. In many banks and building societies, marketing prompted an uncomfortable image of a smooth-talking hustler using canned spiel, the hard sell and half truths to pressure customers into buying products they did not want or need. Such caricatures caused a degree of alienation among branch managers who considered that those activities were not conducive to the role of the professional banker (Berry *et al.* 1989; Turnbull and Wootton 1980).

A fourth difficulty emerged because financial service organisations often lacked appropriately qualified staff with a suitable level of both marketing and technical expertise. It was only when it became apparent that a more effective marketing focus was crucial to future profitability that financial service firms realised that they lacked staff with the requisite skills and experience. To compensate for this lack of expertise many financial service firms have bought in marketing know-how. A key source of this expertise has been industries producing fast-moving consumer goods (de Moubray 1991). In some cases the transition from staff who had a traditional financial service background to retailing experts has been extensive. This scenario is well illustrated in the case of the Trustee Savings Bank. In 1989, after several rounds of rationalisation and restructuring following its Stock Market flotation in October 1986, only three of the bank's twelve most senior executives had traditional financial service backgrounds. The rest had been recruited from other areas of retailing, for example, Ford, Unilever and Proctor and Gamble (*The Economist* 1989a). The lack of qualified and experienced marketing personnel in financial service organisations was a feature identified by Hooley and Mann (1988) even in the late 1980s.

A final factor which has made the moves towards a market-orientated focus difficult has been the organisational structure of many financial service firms. For the most part, market planning and public relations were organised as one function, and advertising as another. Only in the early 1980s were departments restructured to take a strategic overview of all marketing related operations. As Gavaghan (1990: 16) identifies, most decisions relating to 'customer focus, product priority, new product development, pricing and communications' currently originate from bank marketing departments. The way banks have presented their marketing functions has also changed; most consider themselves as financial service providers, as do many other financial service firms. NatWest recently scrapped the position of 'Director of Retail Banking' and replaced it with 'Director of Personal Financial Services' (Meller 1991a).

The ability of financial service firms to adopt a more marketing-orientated focus has not been straightforward, and a number of difficulties have had to be overcome. A well-resourced marketing function is a luxury some financial services institutions have not been able to afford. This feature is most clearly illustrated in the case of building societies. The resources deployed within building society marketing departments vary enormously. In the mid-1980s Newman (1984) undertook a survey of a small, a medium and a large building society. The number of employees located in marketing departments varied enormously: ten, twenty-two, and fifty-five respectively. Recent research by Edgett and Thwaites (1990) of a sample of eighty-one building societies indicated that just over half had a separate marketing department. Of the building societies which did have a distinct marketing department, twenty-five had created the departments in the previous five years. As one might have expected, it was in the larger societies that marketing departments predominated. Despite this patchy coverage, 62 per cent of the building societies indicated that marketing had an impact on all other operations of the business. This final response suggests that while many building societies consider the marketing focus important, many of the smaller societies do not have the resources to support a team of marketing specialists. This point has also been made in relation to the insurance industry. Ford (1990) has argued that deregulation has increased consumer choice, and also reduced the real costs to the consumer. However, fixed costs associated with marketing, such as computer technology and skilled investment management without which companies could not compete effectively, have risen. Small companies who are unable to secure sufficient turnover to cover the higher fixed costs will find it increasingly difficult to compete with larger firms.

In some financial service organisations, the level of sophistication of activities undertaken under the auspices of marketing has also been considered questionable. One such area is the provision of marketing information. As the marketing function expands, the importance of marketing intelligence becomes crucial, as do marketing information systems. Mitchell and Sparks' (1988) study of marketing information systems in five British clearing banks in the late 1980s found that they relied on press clippings, magazines and personal contacts for their market intelligence. Information generated by computer modelling systems was mainly limited to off-the-shelf packages. It was only in the area of market research that banks displayed any degree of sophistication. The larger banks commissioned professional market researchers to collect and analyse their market research, although the smaller banks in the sample did not even engage in this form of rudimentary analysis. A similar conclusion was drawn by Edgett and Thwaites (1990: 46) in relation to the building society industry when they stated 'Market research, sales forecasting and training were found to be lacking in most building societies, both large and small.'

Doubts have also been expressed that financial service firms have used to the best effect the enormous amount of customer information that they have available. The adage '20 per cent of banking customers are profitable but nobody knows which 20 per cent' (Clarke *et al.* 1987: 18) reflects the inability of the banks to target specific customer segments accurately. This problem has occurred because of the accounting practices used within financial institutions which have information systems structured around accounts rather than consumer profiles. As one market researcher has explained, 'Compared with what an insurance company knows about its clients, banks are privy to little more than the current account movements of its customers' (*The Banker* 1988). However, according to research carried out by Bristol University Financial Services Group in 1990, insurance companies fared no better on this issue. It was calculated that less than 25 per cent of the top fifty insurance companies could assess the profitability of different customer segments, and none had comprehensive marketing information systems (Watkins 1992).

It is in the area of relational databases that banks, and some building societies, have been investing considerable resources. The expectation was that customer information presented in a more useful format would assist in cross-selling financial products. However, the financial investment involved in changing filing systems over to the new systems has been enormous, and has cost the banks between £15 and 30 million each. By 1992 NatWest had around 50 per cent, and Midland 60 per cent of its customer details incorporated on relational databases. Both the Abbey National and the Trustee Savings Bank had their systems fully operational by the end of 1992. The building societies have also begun to develop such systems, although at a slower pace than the banks (Watkins 1992). However, it is not clear how some of the smaller financial institutions will be able to purchase and implement such systems, given the considerable financial costs involved.

The trend towards a more market-orientated focus in most areas of the financial services industry is unmistakable, but it would be wrong to conceptualise such moves as an unproblematic activity. Financial firms have had to overcome a range of difficulties, many of which have stemmed from the fact that service marketing management is still an evolving discipline in its own right. The financial costs associated with re-orientating organisations from an overriding emphasis on production to marketing has also proved a critical factor. One of the areas in which financial service firms have invested considerable resources is advertising. The next section assesses the contribution of advertising to the overall marketing effort.

## THE EXPANSION OF FINANCIAL SERVICES ADVERTISING IN THE 1980s AND 1990s

Advertising is not new in the financial services industry. For example, the first advertisement for the Woolwich Building Society took the form of a handbill in 1847. A decade later the Halifax Building Society used a similar strategy. Bank advertising also had a humble beginning. Until the 1920s, bank advertising was almost always linked to crisis and disaster and was 'a symptom less of thriving prosperity than of imminent collapse' (Newman 1984: 307). From the 1920s onwards, banks made attempts to increase awareness of their services. In 1941, the Banking Information Service was established to handle press relations for all the banks. However, even in the advertising of the 1950s there was scepticism at targeting advertising at the working class. For the most part, banks restricted their audience to the well-to-do and the salaried middle class. As Newman (1984: 311) suggests the 'ownership of a bank account and cheque book remained almost a badge of exclusiveness, and was sometimes promoted as such, for existing customers valued this cachet'. The banks' advertising strategy was in contrast to that promoted by the building societies, which were originally set up to provide loans for working-class people to build their own homes. Throughout the 1960s bank audiences were gradually widened. Both Midland and Barclays sponsored films and used cinema advertising. Until the 1970s the use of television advertising was restricted by an inter-bank agreement. After the break up of the bank cartel in 1971, television advertising increased dramatically from 4 per cent to 50 per cent of total bank advertising expenditure in 1980. In 1980 Midland was ranked as the tenth most heavily advertised retailer/brand, as opposed to 131st in 1976 (Newman 1984).

Financial services advertising increased dramatically in the 1980s as the multiplicity of financial service providers and products increased. Throughout the 1980s the financial services sector was the highest spending category, ahead of the traditional high spending categories of food, retailing and motor vehicles. Within the sector, building societies have been the biggest spenders, closely followed by the banks, and then insurance companies. Financial service advertising subsequently became a multi-million pound industry in its own right. Not only have financial service firms spent vast amounts of money on advertising, but they have been more than willing to switch advertising agencies in search of the idiosyncratic ad or catch phrase to capture market share.

However, the turning point came in 1991 when a combined reduction of 18 per cent in press and television expenditure placed the financial services sector in fourth place, down from first place in the previous year. Clearly, the declining profitability of financial institutions had an impact across a range of business functions, marketing activities included. Press advertising has traditionally been the preferred media used by financial services firms because it facilitates more precise targeting of different consumer segments. This is a policy which is still apparent. The largest decline has been in the area of television advertising expenditure, which fell by 26 per cent in 1990–1 (*Marketing* 1992). Middleton (1987) has argued that banks are at a disadvantage compared with some of their non-bank competitors as far as advertising is concerned. Bank marketing budgets have to be distributed over a wide range of products or brands, whereas building societies and insurance companies are able to concentrate advertising on a narrower range of product lines. Essentially banks have been left with the choice between spending larger overall budgets in an attempt to match competitors in different markets, or leave themselves undercommitted in some sectors.

Clearly, the quantity of financial service advertising increased dramatically in the 1980s. However, the nature of financial service advertising also underwent a transformation. In the late 1970s and early 1980s, it concentrated on providing consumers with information about products. From the mid-1980s onwards, financial service advertising strategies focused upon establishing creditability and promoting a user friendly image to attract consumers. Slogans such as 'You're better off talking to us' from Barclays, 'We like to say yes' from TSB, 'The listening bank' from Midland, and 'You get a little Xtra help at the Halifax' were indicative of this change in orientation. The trend in the 1990s has been to combine user friendliness with consumers making demands of financial institutions. The message being conveyed was that consumer wants and needs were of paramount importance. The days when customers had to passively accept what financial service institutions had on offer were over. This was illustrated by Midland Bank's £2 million 'real people' advertising campaign in 1992, when customers were invited in from London's Oxford Street to complain about the bank's services, and service quality (*Marketing* 1992a: 2).

The advertising message propagated by financial institutions was that needs of consumers were being given a higher profile. However, it has been suggested that some financial institutions have promoted images which have been too informal for the type of business transactions undertaken in the industry. This issue was raised by Meller (1991a: 22) when he stated, 'In an attempt to appear approachable, banks have trivialised what is fundamentally important – their position as financial planners and safe places for money. The jocular themes that prevailed in the late 1980s have collided with the way the banks see the future.' On the one hand, banks attempted to dispel their conservative image by providing informal and friendly ads. The problem was that it undermined their future strategy of promoting more higher value added services such as unit trusts, insurance and pensions, which for most people are very serious and important decisions. De Moubray (1991: 68) has pointed out that many financial service advertising campaigns have mistakenly used techniques which have been developed for the promotion of manufactured goods. He has argued that competition has largely been based on price, and there has been insufficient attention paid to the characteristics and properties of services.

Many of the problems financial institutions have confronted in their advertising campaigns are not untypical among other service industries. One of the main problems is that services are intangible. As George and Berry (1981: 55) point out, 'Whereas goods can often be made physically distinctive on the basis of design, packaging, and branding, services have no physical appearance.' In the absence of any concrete visible product which could be used in the ads, financial service firms have endeavoured to appeal to intangible and emotional factors. Ditchburn (1990) has identified two emotional characteristics of successful financial products. The first is that financial products should satisfy consumers' individual ego needs by offering products which have a higher status than those purchased by their peers. Urry (1990: 277) has articulated this situation as 'not so much to keep up with as to differentiate from the Jones'. A second ingredient of success, according to Ditchburn (1990), is the extent to which the possession of a particular financial service product encourages feelings of self-fulfilment; for example, the fact that consumers have managed to purchase a high status account or a lucrative pension.

However, on purchasing financial service products, consumers are not just interested in feeling self-fulfilled, they also want to minimise the risk of a bad choice. This is an issue which applies to financial services more than to most other products because of the horrendous prospect of financial loss. Consumer trust and a company's reputation are both key advertising messages. The problem for advertisers has been that consumer trust and the reputation of a company have been difficult to combine because they can be mutually exclusive. Ford (1990: 23) claims that consumer trust relates to an 'emotional feeling that a company will not let you down', while reputation relates to the view that the company is competent and will provide above-average returns. Research has indicated that while building societies score highly on trust, their reputation only relates to certain products, mainly savings and mortgages. This situation is in direct contrast with insurance companies, whose trust rating is low, but their reputation for making money is high. An important issue for financial institutions in the 1990s will be to find the right balance between reputation and trust.

An additional form of advertising promotion in the 1980s was the massive adoption of incentives. Incentives are not new in the financial service sector. In 1940, Barnard Ellinger remarked on the fact that the banks had introduced 'home safes' which acted as an incentive for customers to save with them. He stated, 'All the banks have now instituted home safes. They provide their customers with small savings boxes free of charge for home safe accounts' (1940: 195). Contemporary incentives differ from earlier attempts in two fundamental ways. First, they are much more widespread than their earlier counterparts, covering a wide range of accounts. Second, it is now usual for incentives to take the form of consumer goods which have absolutely nothing to do with financial services. This is in contrast to the home safes incentive which was directly related to the consumption of financial services by supposedly helping people become better savers.

During the 1980s and 1990s Northbank had introduced various incentives to consumers to buy their financial service products, as had many other financial service organisations. Recent examples include a free push button telephone on the purchase of a Personal Accident Plan, and £25 of free perfume for purchasing a pension plan. At the younger end of the market, discounts on clothes, music and pizzas were a popular option. Many other offers had been introduced over the years involving free petrol, watches, alarm clocks and school equipment in an attempt win over new customers. Perhaps not surprisingly under the circumstances, the segmentation of incentives paralleled the segmentation of different customer groupings. Market segmentation has also been an observable feature of recent product development in the financial services industry.

The next section considers trends in product innovation in the 1980s and 1990s.

## PRODUCT INNOVATION IN THE FINANCIAL SERVICES SECTOR

Product innovation has been used by many firms in recent years as a competitive tool. Producers have competed with each other to generate new and novel services in an attempt to attract more consumers, and in so doing they have speeded up the rate of product development. Harvey (1989: 156) has indicated that the typical half-life of a mass produced, Fordist product was around five to seven years. The advent of post-Fordism has reduced this cycle by half. In some sectors such as video games and computer software, 'the half-life is down to less than eighteen months' (ibid.). The attempts by financial service firms to win new and keep existing customers has substantially widened the choice of accounts available to consumers. For years traditional financial services products were characterised by their simplicity compared with today's standards. Product innovation was a special event, rather than a monthly occurrence. As one commentator of the insurance industry in the 1970s remarked, 'our products have enjoyed life cycles of centuries rather than decades' (Churchill 1972: 153). The rapid product innovation and diversification of the 1980s clearly changed that scenario. Mitchell (1992b: 23) has demonstrated the complexity of the financial service marketplace in relation to the variety of unit trust investments available. He notes, 'There are 23 different categories of unit ... and 151 unit trust management companies. Not every management company has a unit trust in every category, but many categories offer a choice of over 100 different trusts.' Product innovation has also been evident in the banking industry. At the end of the 1980s the major clearing banks produced between 250 and 300 different services (Clarke *et al.* 1988).

Timing and targeting product innovation with accuracy has reaped enormous rewards for some financial service firms. A case in point was in 1984 when Northbank pioneered free banking, aimed at the bank's affluent customers, who objected to paying bank charges while in credit. Around 750,000 consumers transferred their accounts in the twelve months before the competition responded. By contrast, when Lloyds Bank offered its 'Classic' interest bearing current account a few years later, the competition matched the same deal within hours. Banking is a good example of an industry in which product development, and the speed at which it occurs, has become a decisive competitive strategy. One would imagine from such a wide choice of accounts that all consumers' needs could be met. Nevertheless, there were apparently still some customers who complained that Northbank did not offer the combination of services they specifically wanted.

A second feature of recent product innovation in the financial service sector is the introduction of multi-service accounts (first introduced by Midland Bank in the mid-1980s) which incorporated a flexible range of functions. Northbank's multi-service accounts included savings, overdraft, loan, current account and credit card facilities integrated under the umbrella of one account. In effect financial services are being bundled and packaged in a style which resembles simple manufactured products (Watkins and Wright 1986). In theory, the restructuring of accounts has meant that they have become more adaptable to consumers' immediate financial requirements.

The third notable feature is the different ways in which financial services can be delivered. There are an increasing number of ways in which financial service products can be produced and consumed through the use of home banking, telephone banking, ATMs, debit cards, and so on. Banks and building societies have also combined together to provide networks of ATMs. However, co-operation in this way was not the original intention when ATMs were first introduced. As Robinson (1982: 2) indicates, 'Although banks in some countries have entered into ATM development as a co-operative venture, the clearing banks have seen it as a competitive activity.' The original intention was to use ATMs to compete with other financial institutions by providing a superior service. Co-operation only came about when firms considered carefully how expensive such a competitive strategy actually was in practice. The legacy of this competitive intention is reflected in the policy taken collectively by the clearing banks to charge each other a fee when another bank's customer uses their machine. Some building societies have even started passing this fee onto their customers (*Financial Times* 1989). It should be recognised that despite the increase in the number of ATMs, most are situated in larger branches. None of the Northbank sub-branches visited had ATMs installed. This is a situation which contrasts sharply with Rajan's (1987b) vision of sub-branches becoming transformed into hi-tech money shops. If some of the new delivery channels, such as home and telephone banking, were extensively implemented, they could generate wide-ranging changes in consumer behaviour and fundamentally alter the nature of the relationship between financial service organisations and their consumers.

A fourth feature of product innovation in the 1980s is market segmentation. Financial institutions realised in the 1980s what other retailers had learnt in the 1960s, that all buyers have individual needs. The use of segmentation variables included income, age, employment classification, stage in the life cycle, lifestyle and housing tenure. Geodemographic information systems such as ACORN (A Classification of Residences and Neighbourhoods) were also used to analyse household segments on the basis of their property location, and thus facilitate the precise targeting of direct mail campaigns. In fact the extensive use of geo-demographic information among financial service institutions has led to them being the most active users of the systems (Sleight 1992). Financial service institutions have used market segmentation to identify more precisely the financial needs of particular groups of the population, and have then constructed products which match those needs. For example, a life cycle analysis of financial service needs would acknowledge that families and individuals at different stages in the life cycle have different financial requirements. The segment described as 'full nest 1' is one in which the youngest child is under 6 years of age. The emphasis would probably be on building up the family home, and the household is likely to be short of cash. Channon (1987: 9) indicates that people within this market segment tend to be interested in newly advertised products, either home- or child-related. The needs of 'full nest 1' are in contrast to those of young bachelors who usually have 'few financial burdens, are interested in fashion and leisure activities and, as a consequence will be active purchasers of vacations, sporty cars and mating game equipment'. One of the most recent segmentation variables to be used is lifestyle. The 1980s spawned a whole range of lifestyle classifications such as yuppies (young, upwardly progressing individuals), dinkies (dual income, no kids individuals) and glams (greying, leisured, affluent marrieds). The result of segmentation strategies has been to specifically target financial services at groups of individuals, rather than for indiscriminate mass consumption. The benefit as far as consumers are concerned is that they are able to choose services which are tailored to suit their individual needs.

Financial institutions, in common with many other retailers, also began to promote products which were 'green' and ethically sound in an attempt to attract additional consumers. A particularly high profile campaign was the Co-operative Bank's ethical policy adopted in May 1992. The charter indicated that the bank:

- 'will not invest or supply financial services to any regime or organisation which oppresses the human spirit, takes away the rights of individuals or manufactures any instrument of torture;

- will not finance or in any way facilitate the manufacture or sale of weapons to any country which has an oppressive regime;
- will not invest in any business involved in animal experimentation for cosmetic purposes;
- will not support any person or company using exploitative factory farm methods;
- will not engage in business with any farm or other organisation engaged in the production of animal fur;
- will not support any organisation involved in blood sports;
- will not provide financial services to tobacco manufacturers' (see Co-operative Bank 1992 for additional policy statements).

Several banks introduced affinity credit cards which had links with charities. Most schemes involved the card issuer paying an initial contribution to the respective nominated organisation, and thereafter contributing an amount based on card turnover, usually 25 pence per £100. Examples of such partnerships included the Bank of Scotland and the NSPCC, the Trustee Savings Bank and Save the Children Fund, and Giro Bank teamed up with Oxfam (Ellwood 1989). There has also been a substantial increase in the number of unit trust funds which invest in green and ethically sound companies (*Investors Chronicle* 1993). All the signs are that ethical trusts have been a good investment. Between July 1991 and July 1992 investment in general unit trusts increased by 3 per cent in comparison with over 17 per cent for ethical trusts. So great has the demand been for ethical unit trusts that it may become difficult for fund managers to find suitable companies in which to invest in future. Financial institutions who do not offer ethical products in their portfolio may be missing out on important marketing opportunities in the future (Ennew and McKechnie 1992).

Finally, in the 1980s Northbank, along with many other financial service organisations, had transformed its product range by the use of branding. The branding of goods has been a facility available to manufacturers in Britain for over a century, while the facility only became available for services since 1986 (Murphy 1990). Since the legislation came into effect, financial services firms have scrambled to brand their services (Taylor 1987). Blackett (1991) has indicated that the need for coherent branding strategies in financial services emerged for two main reasons. First, it enables producers to differentiate themselves from each other in a crowded marketplace following deregulation. Second, it differentiates the variety of products emerging on the financial service scene. A proliferation of brands promptly ensued, such as Liquid

Gold, the high interest savings accounts introduced by the Leeds Permanent Building Society, Leading Edge pensions from Abbey Life, and Freedom life insurance from Guardian Royal Exchange, among many others.

Successful branding opens up the possibility to add value to goods and services. Murphy (1990) has suggested that branding operates at the level of a pact between producers and consumers which develops over time. Branding embraces sets of values and attributes which differentiate one brand from similar products and services. However, there are more difficulties with branding services because of their intangibility, and because they are often in a constant state of flux. A company such as Coca-Cola can be relatively confident that they have a successful brand which could remain the same for the next twenty years. In the financial services industry, however, companies can be forced to make substantial changes at relatively short notice. These adjustments may be a response to legislative change, interest rate fluctuations and other fiscal measures.

Branding initiatives are not without their risks, and it has been estimated that nineteen out of twenty brands fail (Murphy 1990). Many of the successful brands such as Marlboro, Pepsi and Kellogg benefited from investment in brand building in the 1950s and 1960s, when advertising was inexpensive by today's standards. Many world class brands such as Coca-Cola, Kodak and Shell have been around for 100 years or more. Financial service firms have not benefited from any of these advantages. They have attempted to brand a whole range of services as quickly as possible, and at a time when advertising was expensive. Consequently, not all attempts at branding financial services have been successful.

Northbank had been at the forefront of product diversification and branding in an attempt to differentiate its products from those of other organisations. However, the result was often confusion among both staff and consumers. The extent of product innovation was so great that staff had to undergo special monthly product training sessions to keep them up-to-date on new initiatives (see Chapter 4). Employees commented on the amount of time they had to spend explaining the key features and functions of different financial products to consumers. The branding strategy employed by many financial service firms necessitated a high degree of financial sophistication on the part of consumers. It is not clear that all consumers are financially well-educated enough to discern the variations between different financial products. This is particularly the case in the area of investment products because they are often 'one-off' purchases. The problem of confusion among consumers as a result of branding and diversification strategies has been acknowledged by some financial institutions. After a decade of product branding, in the early 1990s Midland Bank reversed its policy. Instead, the bank intended to concentrate on supplying a smaller number of simpler products, and to promote the corporate, rather than individual brands (Meller 1991b).

Product diversification and branding were areas in which financial service institutions invested heavily in the 1980s. However, the most visible evidence that organisations were attempting to promote a more consumer-orientated focus was the refurbishment of their high street and town centre premises. The reorganisation of the physical environment in which services are produced and consumed is the theme of the final section of the chapter.

## THE SERVICE DELIVERY AND THE SEGMENTATION OF THE PHYSICAL ENVIRONMENT

Within the services marketing literature, there has been a growing awareness of the importance of the physical environment in which the service delivery occurs. Bateson (1992) has argued that because many services are delivered in surroundings which have been created by the service firm, the environment itself becomes part of the product design. The physical environment thus contributes to the perceived 'personality' and image of an organisation. This allows the service environment to be used as an important differentiating factor in a highly competitive marketplace. Furnishings, equipment, stationery, general decoration, colour, lighting, space, shape, texture of materials, and employees all provide 'cues' to the style, status, consumer orientation and personality of the organisation. The uniformity of the physical environment is desirable for a number of important reasons. First, it encourages consumers to identify with the image of the organisation, and hopefully to investigate the possibility of purchasing a service. Second, it enables organisations to advertise nationally in a standardised way. Finally, it attempts to provide psychological reassurance to customers that whatever branch of the organisation they are in, the environment feels familiar (Cowell 1984).

The effect of atmospherics, or the physical environment in which a service takes place, has been considered crucial by managers in relation to how a service is perceived by consumers. Despite this concern, there has been little empirical research which has directly addressed the impact of the physical surroundings, or 'servicescape', on the consumption process (Bitner 1992: 57). Nevertheless, the physical use of space gives important indications to the status of different activities within an organisation. Bateson (1992) has expressed this dichotomy as one between operations and marketing. The operations perspective has stressed the use of space in terms of the ability to house physical plant which is crucial to the production process. By contrast, the marketing perspective has given a higher profile to the impact of the physical environment on the activities of consumers.

Financial institutions have not been renowned for their inviting, user-friendly premises, and this is especially true of British banks. In the nineteenth century, in the days when banks frequently went bust, banks were built in an architectural style which promoted a solid, secure, and conservative image. As Kay (1987: 159) notes, 'the older branches look like miniature versions of the Bank of England, complete with granite pillars and windows too high to let anyone see in'. The internal decor, which often consisted of intricately carved mahogany and marble, evoked the quality, substance and style of service which was available only to a particular elite group, rather than the mass market. The early banks projected a middle-class image which reflected the market segment they were trying to attract (Booker 1991). However, even in this setting, the spatial layout of the branches highlighted the fact that issues relating to production were given priority over those of consumption. Staff occupied around 90 per cent of the total office space, leaving customers with something in the region of 10 per cent. More often than not, the available space consisted of standing room in long, narrow and somewhat bare banking halls, where customers submissively waited before having the 'pleasure' of being served.

This image of the bank branch has not gone down too well with the consumers of the 1980s and 1990s. To a large extent they have voted with their feet to the benefit of similar financial service organisations, especially the building societies, who have promoted a less formal and a more friendly image. Having realised their staid image was not entirely appropriate in an era of intense competition, the banks have endeavoured to make their branches more customer friendly. There has been a concerted effort to break down barriers, to dispel the austere image in favour of one which places emphasis on a relaxed and pleasant atmosphere. This transformation has been approached in a number of ways. More open plan branches have developed, with the bulk of the floorspace being used as public space for consumers rather than producers. Comfortable seating areas, potted palms and even Lego for children are all symbolic of the recognition of the increased consumer orientation. So is the design of some of the new or refurbished branches which have large plate glass shop windows rather than blank frontages and frosted glass. As Howcroft and Lavis (1986: 203) have revealed, though, the corporate identity is still never very far away, portrayed by a 'panoply of visual symbols and colours that identify branches by the fascia, advertisements, by their logo and typeface, and all the promotional and administrative activities of the organisation'. The ultimate aim has been to entice customers inside by displaying a welcoming and appealing environment. This style and layout have been copied by financial institutions from retailers along the road to promoting money shops and financial supermarkets. Financial institutions have become well aware that consumers who are not satisfied with any aspect of the service delivery could take their business elsewhere. The physical environment has become a useful indicator in determining whether organisations have taken a consumer-led approach seriously.

In a similar way to many other financial service organisations, Northbank's branches were concentrated in town centre or prominent high street sites. This is a feature which is related to the prestige, status and visibility of the organisation as much as consumer demand (Whysall 1989). Most branches were situated in primary sites directly surrounded by other financial service providers. However, what might have been a prime site at one historical moment is not necessarily still so after several rounds of spatial restructuring. It was noticeable that one branch had been slightly separated from the locus of activity within the town centre because the centre had actually moved. As a consequence, the branch had been downgraded to a sub-branch in preparation for closure a few months later. In its place the bank had clinched a deal for a site right in the hub of the town centre next to Marks & Spencer. This was obviously a prime opportunity for attracting passing trade. Finding the right site has become an increasingly prominent activity in banking, as in other consumer and producer services, and is an area of strategy which needs constant review. Indeed it has become a specialist industry in its own right, whereby consultants give advice and guidance on location strategy (*Banking Technology* 1989).

As far as branch refurbishment is concerned, Northbank has been at the forefront of the revolution in creating the 'designer branch'. However, it has been the inside of the branches rather than the outside which have been given prominence. From the outside many of the branches do not look significantly different from when they were first built in the nineteenth and early twentieth century, apart from the use of colour on the bank's logo and the odd posters on the windows. All of Northbank's branches have recently undergone internal refurbishment using designer carpet, and the bank's logo has been displayed at every opportunity. Overall, the branches have become much less formal and consumer friendly, mainly through the use of brighter colours. In some of the branches the dark mahogany counters have been replaced with ones in a much lighter wood, similar to the colour of furniture consumers might have in their own home. Comfortable seating has been incorporated into public spaces, which have been 'opened up' and which usually contain one of the bank's counsellors to provide advice and guidance on the bank's services. In some of the larger branches, which have the space, ATMs have been installed to enable customers to service themselves.

The transition from the old to the new style branch was a slow process, and for some the re-design was not possible. Many of the branches, particularly sub-branches in the suburbs, still retain their old mahogany counters, wood panelling and the traditional writing desk. The costly nature of refurbishment has meant that sub-branches were last on the list. This suggests that complete refurbishment tended to err on the side of wishful thinking rather than reality. However, there were other constraints besides those of a financial nature. Not unlike 10–12 per cent of all clearing bank branches, two of the Northbank branches visited had listed building status which limited the extent of alterations which could be undertaken (Newman 1984). There was also considerable opposition from local pressure groups. In one case, the Victorian Society scrutinised plans put forward for council approval and protested against those they considered inappropriate. Because of this policing, only the inside of one of the branches could be re-designed. The other listed branch could not be altered either inside or out, and was totally inappropriate in the age of the consumer branch. Because of the problems associated with structural change, the branch was closed down altogether. It was somewhat surprising that a few months later the listed building was re-opened as a public house, with the entirely approriate name of the 'Counting House'!

The aim of much redevelopment in the 1980s was undoubtedly to make banks more approachable, but had the additional benefit of providing an appropriate atmosphere in which employees could sell bank services. At the end of the 1980s, Northbank had spent millions of pounds on their branch re-design programme, which was based on zones to enhance the opportunity for selling various financial products. As customers entered the branches they were met by the first zone consisting of ATMs which enable customers to service themselves. The second zone included receptionists and counsellors who assisted with simple enquiries. The third zone took the form of interview rooms, where employees sold complex products in a confidential environment.

Clearly financial institutions, especially the banks, have incurred considerable costs in their attempts to become more consumer-orientated. How successful refurbishment programmes have been is difficult to quantify with any degree of accuracy. Research by NatWest in the mid-1980s indicated that people perceived a greater difference between branches of the same bank than they did between banks. This probably means that NatWest, and other financial institutions, have not achieved a uniformity of public response accorded to other high street retailers (Kay 1987).

## CONCLUSION

It is clear that financial institutions have gone to great lengths to attract consumers. Marketing was a relatively peripheral function until the 1980s, but has expanded rapidly since deregulation. Financial institutions have spent vast amounts of money on advertising in an attempt to persuade consumers to purchase their products. Product diversification and branding were all designed to offer consumers something novel, new and different. Branch premises were also re-designed to promote a more consumer-friendly environment.

Despite these considerable efforts, the process has not been a straight-forward case of producers manipulating consumers. Problems have occurred because of the newness of services marketing, and the difficulties of promoting an immaterial service, as opposed to a physical, manufactured product. Financial service firms have not always used the information they had about consumers in a particularly effective way. Even in the late 1980s and early 1990s, few firms were able to accurately identify the profitability of different consumer segments. Attempts at diversification and branding were designed to give consumers a wider choice of products, and to enable consumers to identify different products more easily. However, all too often consumers have been confused by the vast array of different services available. Finally, the attempts by firms to re-design their branches have been met by resistance from local interest groups. The extensive financial resources required by refurbishment programmes has also meant that a relatively small number of branches have benefited.

Financial service firms have found it increasingly difficult to differentiate themselves from other financial service providers since deregulation in the mid-1980s. They all tend to produce similar products, at similar prices. One strategy which firms have attempted to use to differentiate themselves is service quality. This places an increased premium on the quality of financial service staff in their interaction with consumers. Some of the ways in which financial service firms have attempted to operationalise service quality will be assessed in the next chapter.

## SUMMARY

**Financial service institutions went to considerable lengths to attract new and retain existing consumers in the 1980s and 1990s. They have:**

1  **developed their marketing information systems;**
2  **vastly expanded their advertising programmes;**
3  **engaged in product innovation and branding;**
4  **and reorganised the physical environment in which the service delivery takes place.**

# Chapter 4

# Service quality, marketing, and human resource management strategies

Financial services institutions tend to provide comparable services at similar prices. The ability of organisations to gain competitive advantage by the use of product differentiation is limited, because financial service products can be copied within a relatively short space of time. The demystification of some financial services, has also meant that consumers are not as easily persuaded by the implied perceptual differences between products created through advertising (Tarver 1987). Instead, financial organisations have attempted to use service quality to gain competitive advantage, by persuading consumers that they offer a more superior service than their competitors. Service quality has become much more of an issue in recent years because of higher consumer expectations, whether they be in relation the physical environment in which the service occurs, the reliability of technology used during transactions, or the service provided by employees (Lewis 1989). However, because of the labour intensive nature of most service provision, a great deal of the literature relating to quality in the service sector has focused on the human interaction within the service delivery.

The objective of this chapter is to assess to what extent and in what ways human resource management policies have been used by financial service organisations to promote a more consumer orientated culture, by emphasising the issue of service quality. Prior to the 1980s, financial service organisations provided consumers with a relatively narrow range of financial service products. Providing a quality service, and expertise in an extensive range of financial products, to larger numbers of consumers is relatively new. It is not clear how financial service staff have reacted to this re-orientation, or how human resource management policies have been used to support this change in organisational culture. Financial service organisations have had to recognise that if they are to remain profit able, customers' needs should be satisfied in-house rather than by competitors.

Customer-centred marketing has become an increasingly crucial part of the financial service delivery. The implementation of perform ance related pay has been introduced by many financial service firms to reinforce the 'new' marketing focus. It is not clear how financial service staff have reacted to these changes in their job description. As in the previous chapter, a range of examples will be drawn from the case study of Northbank (see Appendix), in addition to other financial service organisations.

## SERVICE QUALITY: SOME IMPLICATIONS FOR HUMAN RESOURCE MANAGEMENT

The labour factor in service organisations is particularly important because of the labour intensive nature of most service provision (Gershuny and Miles 1983). In addition to being labour intensive, service occupations often require a high degree of visibility by employees. De Moubray (1985) has estimated that 90 per cent of staff working in service industries have direct contact with customers, as opposed to 10 per cent in manufacturing. The importance of front-line employees in providing this personalised, quality service is vividly articulated by Jan Carlzon's (1987) expression 'moments of truth', describing the point at which consumer expectations of the service delivery are fulfilled, or disappointed. The emphasis on the quality of interaction between organisations and their consumers has stimulated the emergence of a new organisational theory. Service Management, is a concept on which the massive increase in customer care programmes have been based (Albrecht and Zemke 1985; Brown 1991).

Customer care became a buzz word within financial service organisations in the 1980s, as it did in many other industries in Britain. Research by Smith and Lewis (1989) found that the use of customer care programmes in the financial services sector was extensive. The two main reasons for their introduction within banks and building societies were first to differentiate themselves from other similar organisations, and second because of increasing competition. The main reason for their implementation in the insurance industry was to improve staff attitudes towards consumers. Several rounds of re-organistion and cost-cutting had resulted in a lowering of staff morale and service quality. It was hoped that customer care/service programmes would alleviate the 'anti-customer' service ethos which had developed.

The philosophy underlying customer care/service policies has rested upon the assumption that there are characteristics which consumers recognise as being indicative of a superior service delivery. There have been several attempts to provide broad frameworks which integrate key elements of a 'successful' service delivery from the consumers' perspective (see Mersha and Adlakha 1992). Urry (1986: 9) has suggested that receivers of a particular service expect 'efficiency, friendliness, but not over friendliness, not to be patronised, not to be sexually or physically threatened, predictability and accountability'. Parasuraman *et al.* (1985) have also identified ten dimensions of service quality: accessibility, reliability, responsiveness, competence, courtesy, communication, credibility, security, understanding/knowing the consumer, and tangible cues, such as the physical environment in which the service is delivered. Nevertheless, conceptualising what individual consumers want from their relationship with producers is a highly subjective process. Surprenant and Solomon's (1985) research relating to the personalisation of the service delivery demonstrated that individual consumers gave priority to a diverse range of characteristics. For example, an employee's manner which appears friendly and helpful to one consumer, may be considered intrusive and off-putting by another. Research has also indicated that there are important cultural differences in consumer expectations of the service delivery. In a recent comparative study, Lewis (1991) assessed bank customers' expectations and perceptions of service quality in the UK and US. As far as consumers in the UK were concerned, they placed a high premium on

> privacy, interior and staff appearances, and using customer suggest-ions to improve service; and US respondents were more concerned about location and parking, opening hours, the number of staff available to serve (with associated perceptions of slow-moving queues), and several of the personal characteristics of bank staff they came into contact with.
>
> (Lewis 1991: 60)

Overall, the sample of bank consumers in the UK and the US were generally 'satisfied or very satisfied' with the service quality they received.

Despite the variability between consumers' perceptions of a successful service delivery, it appears that service managers believe a happy, smiling employee is a crucial ingredient. Some financial service firms have gone to great lengths to project this aspect of the service delivery. In 1989 NatWest's US retail division was so convinced of the quality of its staff–consumer interaction that it launched a $2.5 million advertising campaign which informed its customers that it 'would cough up $5 if they were greeted by a grunt rather than a polite "hello" ' (*The Economist* 1989b: 87). NatWest tried a similar programme in the UK, but without the misery money guarantee. Austrin (1990) has cited a similar example in a New Zealand bank. He describes a situation where managers placed a goldfish bowl full of 10 cent pieces on the counter in front of each teller position. A sign encouraged customers to help themselves from the bowl if the cashier did not greet them with a smile. The smiling face scenario is not only a feature of the human service delivery either. Channon (1987) cites examples of ATMs in the US and Japan which have been programmed to provide customer assistance along with a picture of a friendly girl smiling. However, some financial institutions, especially building societies, have deliberately underutilised the self-service technology available in an attempt to promote a friendly image, of which the personal service is a key component (Rajan and Cooke 1986).

These examples indicate support for Hochschild's (1983) view that employees are increasingly having to learn to be more pleasing and attentive to the needs of consumers, earning such work the label of 'emotional labour'. Swan and Coombs (1976) support this view when they state that the expressive element of the service delivery is more important than the technical competence exhibited by the service provider. They illustrate this viewpoint by giving the example of a customer obtaining a loan. While a customer may be impressed by the speed and efficiency of the bank sanctioning the loan, the consumer may have taken exception to the manner in which they were attended to by bank personnel. The experience of a poor service delivery would therefore reduce the overall level of satisfaction with the service. This leads Buswell (1986) to conclude, that a measure of the quality of consumer–producer interaction in service organisations should be biased towards expressive rather than technical skills.

An acknowledgement of the importance of interpersonal skills relative to technical skills had been the driving force behind a recent re-evaluation of the occupational structure at Northbank. Previously, the hierarcical grading of specific occupations was based upon the technical skills required by employees to do the job. More recently, however, there has been a shift towards ranking occupations in terms of the degree of communication skills required to complete the job effectively. For example, the job of a standing order clerk is not that demanding in relation to the technical know-how required, but it is an area which had consistently generated customer complaints. Because of the need to resolve consumer problems effectively, the job has been ranked at a higher grade than had previously been the case, and is staffed by more experienced personnel. Similarly, chief cashiers who were responsible for the smooth operation of the counter service have been either promoted or more qualified staff have been employed in that position in an attempt to provide a superior service to consumers. Changes in the occupational structure at Northbank are indicative of a trend to concentrate experienced staff in problem-resolution positions, in an attempt to improve service quality.

The specialisation of financial service employees has been another way in which organisations have attempted to promote service quality. In many financial institutions there has been a division between corporate, small business and retail financial services. There has also been a degree of specialisation within retail banking. Barclays' notion of the 'personal banker' is indicative of this trend, as are positions such as mortgage adviser, student adviser and consumer counsellor. However, whether specialist staff provide a higher quality of service is questionable. This issue has been assessed by Howcroft and Hill (1992) in relation to service quality in the mortgage market. They found that the use of specialists rather than a general enquiry desk reduced the length of time consumers had to wait before being attended to. However, neither the length of waiting time nor the use of specialist personnel was a good indicator of service quality. The institution that had the longest waiting time and used a general enquiry desk provided the most informative and professional service.

Another strategy employed by financial institutions was the use of district service centres, or paper factories, where most of the data generated by branches was processed in a central location. While the concept is relatively new to Britain, the concentration of data processing into specialist centres has been implemented for some time in the US, France, and Australia (Bertrand and Noyelle 1988; Williams 1988; O'Reilly 1992). Along with other banks and building societies, in the late 1980s Northbank introduced a system of 12 district processing centres. The bank took the view that expensive high street premises were not the place for undertaking routine data processing. Rather, more time and space needed to be made available for employees to spend time providing a quality service for customers and marketing bank services. The data processing centres also provided an efficient service for corporate consumers who were in receipt of large numbers of cheques because of the 24-hour processing that the centres provided.

Clearly, service quality is an important way in which organisations can differentiate themselves from each other. However, it has also been argued that service quality can also improve the level of profitability within organisations. According to Buzzell and Gale (1987: 107) 'Whether the profit measure is return on sales or return on investment, businesses with a superior product/service offering clearly out-perform those with inferior quality.' They highlight several strategic advantages that were gained by firms who succeeded in providing a quality service to consumers in terms of: customer loyalty; increased repeat business; ability to command a relatively higher price without losing market share; lower marketing costs; and growth in market share. Reichheld and Sasser (1990) have argued that improvements in service quality should be considered an investment rather than a cost. One financial service organisation in Britain which has reaped considerable rewards from pursuing a total quality management strategy is Girobank. Since 1987 the bank has implemented a programme which focused on three areas: quality improvement, customer care, and quality assurance. Tangible benefits have been a 52 per cent reduction in keyboard operator errors, a 25 per cent reduction in customer complaints, and a 38 per cent reduction in inventory. The bank has estimated that savings from quality improvement projects have exceeded £6 million, and £2.6 million has been saved through implementing staff suggestions. Furthermore, positive customer perceptions of Girobank have increased significantly (Henderson 1992).

The need to get things right first time, or very right the second time, has become of paramount importance in service industries (Berry and Parasuraman 1991). Crosby (1985) has estimated that the costs of poor quality in manufacturing organisations can account for between 25–30 per cent of sales turnover, while in services the figure is even higher at 40–50 per cent. Even an accuracy rate of 98 per cent in a large organisation may have the effect of generating thousands of mistakes which need rectifying. Another cost of poor service quality is an adverse word-of-mouth rating by consumers. Berry *et al.* (1989) have argued that dissatisfied consumers tell nine to ten people about an unhappy experience; this is reduced to around five individuals if the problem is handled satisfactorily. Negative word of mouth may impede the cross-selling of services to existing customers and also discourage new or potential customers. However, the true cost of poor service quality may never be known. Estimates suggest that around 30 per cent of customers who experience a service problem never complain. Similarly, Singh and Pandya's (1991) research of consumer dissatisfaction of bank and other financial services (excluding insurance) revealed that the relationship between consumer dissatisfaction and the incidence of complaining was weak. This presents a problem for service managers, because customer dissatisfaction can only be systematically managed when customers voice their complaints. The costs associated with losing consumers are difficult to quantify with any degree of accuracy because contemporary accounting systems are not generally designed to capture the value of customer loyalty. For the most part, 'systems focus on current period costs and revenues and ignore cash flows over a customer's lifetime' (Reichheld and Sasser 1990: 106). That said, the estimated cost of losing a customer has been calculated by Midland Bank. Midland's marketing manager has stated 'The lifetime value of each customer from student through ABC1 to retirement is over £100,000 in commissions and fees. To lose him or her is the real cost question' (*Marketing* 1992b: 2).

An important challenge confronted by financial institutions has been the provision of a quality service for consumers. Another feature of a quality service delivery has been to ensure consumers' needs are fulfilled in-house rather than elsewhere. The extent to which financial service staff have been motivated to change from roles that were essentially administrative to ones which involve person-to-person marketing is an important issue, and one which has wide-ranging implications for training.

## THE TRAINING IMPLICATIONS OF A MARKET ORIENTATED FOCUS

The transition from administrative to interpersonal and marketing skills is not just a feature of employment practices in the financial services sector in Britain. Bertrand and Noyelle's (1988) study of financial service institutions, including banks and insurance companies in the US, Japan and Europe, indicated that administrative and procedural competence was being replaced by customer assistance and sales skills. A similar argument has been advanced by Hirschhorn (1985), who has suggested that information technology has been crucial in changing the boundary between producers and consumers. The extensive use of technology has transformed the bank employees' role from one which involved servicing customers' routine needs to one involving proactively marketing and selling financial products. As a result of this reorganisation the tenor of the relationship between producers and consumers moves from one of politeness and support to an aggressive proactive battleground, with the customer as the sales target.

However, it is not clear whether existing financial services staff will be able to make the necessary transition. Prior to the 1980s, banks and building societies did not strategically recruit sales orientated staff. This has been reflected in the terms and conditions of their employment, which have usually included a regular salary, a career structure, profit sharing, a subsidised mortgage and various other perks. This is in sharp contrast to insurance salespeople who have tended to have a low basic salary, but with a significant commission on sales. The traditional method of communicating with the market, particularly by branch managers, has tended to be through the participation in community affairs and giving speeches which were geared to inform rather than sell. The atmosphere of the personal contact was one of counsellor and client, not of the buyer and seller of bank services (Rathmell 1974). Berry *et al.* (1985: 3) have suggested that in the past it tended to be 'salesmanship through the media rather than through people. Bank employees were order takers. Their job was to fulfil the requests that advertising, public relations and promotions encouraged. It was ads that sold not people.' It was the customer who sold themselves to the bank, rather than the other way around. According to Berry and Thompson (1982), relationship banking is fundamentally different from order-taking, where the focus lies with the employees selling specific services to customers. The relationship banking approach concentrates on clients', rather than customers', individual needs and how those needs might be satisfied. In essence, 'Good service is crucial to relationship retention. Good selling is crucial to relationship enhancement' (Berry and Thompson 1982: 65).

The changing relationship between employees and consumers is one which financial service firms have had to cultivate and manage through staff development initiatives. The importance of employee training in supporting this change in organisational culture has been crucial. However, it has been a daunting task to organise because of the large numbers of staff involved and the geographically dispersed nature of many financial service organisations. That said, the financial services sector has a good record on training by comparison with other sectors of the British economy. The Labour Force Survey in 1991 indicated that only in the category 'other services' did employees receive more training than staff in the financial services sector (cited in Turner *et al.* 1992). However, it needs to be recognised that the financial services sector covers a number of industries, each with their own distinctive training orientation. The level of training in the insurance industry has recently received a great deal of criticism in Britain. Cross-national research which has assessed the training of clerical employees in the banking industry has also demonstrated that British staff are not as well trained as some of their European contemporaries (Lane 1987; O'Reilly 1992).

Northbank has made active strides in its staff training programmes to prepare its employees for a more consumer-orientated role. All of Northbank's employees have attended in-house training courses which focused on selling bank products, and all have been on a two-day 'Putting Customers First' course presented by outside consultants. However, the main systematic and sustained training which employees received was through the bank's product knowledge training scheme which also operated as a quality circle. The usefulness of quality circles in Britain has been heightened by the increasing competitiveness of Japanese manufacturing firms during the 1980s, which tended to use them as part of total quality management programmes. Collard and Dale's (1985) survey of quality circles in Britain indicated that the reason for their implementation in manufacturing firms was to improve employees' job satisfaction, while in service organisations the development of employees was most important. Northbank was one of the first British banks to introduce quality circles, which occurred in the mid-1980s. This was at a later stage than Japanese banks, where they were introduced in the 1970s (Watanabe 1990).

Northbank took a fairly standard approach to quality circles. Usually teams of around six to eight staff met together, headed by a team leader who discussed the salient points of new services, utilising booklets and videos. During meetings employees were encouraged to indicate which financial service products should be sold to particular consumers, and in what situations. The quality circles at Northbank were highly focused on marketing and selling, unlike those in other service organisations which are often more broadly based (Dale 1986). Most employees at Northbank felt that the quality circles training was useful because it kept them up-to-date about new product ranges being developed and marketed by the bank. From Northbank's point of view, quality circles helped to promote an aspect of corporate culture which focused on selling by using team work, common goals, and a competition league. However, the scheme did have several disadvantages. One of the main problems was that it was very time consuming. Difficulties in organising meetings because of lunch breaks, sickness, staff training, or the sheer pressure of work meant that some branches could not complete the quality circle modules at the appropriate times. It was therefore conceivable that customers could ask for information about a particular service which members of staff knew nothing about. The fact that the same teams could not always meet together also meant the group cohesion, integral to the scheme, was broken.

Despite the increase in sales training, it was not clear that financial service staff wanted to switch from a role that was predominantly administrative to one which included both marketing and administration. Likewise, not all employees want to be committed to enter into the type of relationship with customers required of them by their employers. In some instances, employees may be faced with a conflict of interest between what is best for the organisation in which they work and the most beneficial course of action for consumers. This situation occurs because in many ways front-line employees have 'boundary-spanning roles' and are as close, psychologically and physically, to the organisation's customers as they are to fellow employees (Bowen and Schneider 1985). While the employer might wish staff to sell financial products as frequently as possible, employees may feel uncomfortable in that role, especially if they believe the sale is not entirely in the consumer's best interest.

Given the obvious importance of the service delivery, and in particular the marketing element involved in the cross-selling of bank services, the research at Northbank questioned employees about their attitudes towards marketing and the amount of time spent on marketing related activities. These aspects of change will be discussed in the next section.

## TELLERS INTO SELLERS? PERSONAL SELLING IN FINANCIAL INSTITUTIONS

When constructing a personal selling strategy for its employees, a firm has the choice between using full-time or part-time marketing personnel. According to Gummesson's (1991) definition, part-time marketeers carry out marketing activities but do not belong to a sales or marketing department. The part-time marketeer approach recognises that large numbers of employees have face-to-face contact with customers, but that they are not necessarily salespeople. The part-time marketeer strategy facilitates the distribution of the marketing function throughout the organisation via employees whose main duties are concerned with other tasks or functions (Gronroos 1990). Northbank has chosen the part-time marketeer strategy, and marketing has been added to the job descriptions of all employees. Employees are now conscripted as part-time marketeers whether they like it or not.

The move towards more of a marketing focus has been extensive at Northbank. The bank has begun to send out mailshots, engage in telesales, and promote their products through special events such as investment evenings and visits to workplaces and schools. Many of Northbank's clerical employees commented that more 'sophisticated consumers' were 'shopping around' financial service organisations in order to get the best deal. In some instances this included bringing in another organisation's leaflet and showing it to bank staff as an example

*Table 4.1* Percentage of Northbank's employees who enjoyed marketing

| Response | Grade* of employee | | | | | Total % |
| | 2 | 3 | 4 | 5 | Managerial | |
| --- | --- | --- | --- | --- | --- | --- |
| Yes | 6 | 12 | 18 | 8 | 10 | 54 |
| No | – | 6 | – | – | – | 6 |
| Sometimes | – | 16 | 10 | 8 | 6 | 40 |
| Total | 6 | 34 | 28 | 16 | 16 | 100 |

*Source:* Burton (1992); sample based on the reponses of fifty employees.
*Note:* *Grade refers to the grading structure used by UK clearing banks, grade 2 being the lowest and grade 5 the highest clerical level.

of the competition. This has placed a lot of pressure on bank staff to sell and give advice on Northbank's services and how they differ from what other providers in the market have to offer.

Marketing had also become an important feature of managerial work. Throughout the 1980s there was a series of early retirement deals for branch managers who did not want to be involved with marketing and selling. It was significant that many managers took the opportunity to leave. Within the Northbank Area Office, which included twenty-two branch managers, there was not one branch manager in the area who had been in a branch managerial post ten years previously. Senior management at Northbank considered that the older, more experienced managers were not able to adapt to the new marketing focus. However, this assumption is contradicted by Otley (1991). In his sample of bank managers, the older managers accepted the increased marketing profile more readily than younger managers. Nevertheless, as a result of the shift in emphasis at Northbank, most of the new branch managers were much younger and less experienced than had previously been the case. For the most part, recently appointed managers had been given the job because they had proven marketing expertise.

The attitudes of clerical employees towards marketing and selling was more varied. Around 54 per cent of Northbank's employees indicated that they enjoyed marketing, while 40 per cent replied that they sometimes enjoyed the activity (Table 4.1). Employees were also questioned about whether or not they were confident when marketing bank products to customers. Around 54 per cent indicated that they were confident, while 42 per indicated sometimes, and only 4 per cent gave a negative response (Table 4.2). Managers remarked that it was some of the longer serving employees who had difficulties in adapting, or who had even resisted the

*Table 4.2* Percentage of Northbank's employees who were confident when marketing services

| Confidence rating | Grade of employee | | | | | Total % |
|---|---|---|---|---|---|---|
| | 2 | 3 | 4 | 5 | Managerial | |
| Yes | 4 | 12 | 14 | 12 | 12 | 54 |
| Sometimes | 2 | 18 | 14 | 4 | 4 | 42 |
| No | | 4 | | | | 4 |
| Total | 6 | 34 | 28 | 16 | 16 | 100 |

*Source:* Burton (1992); sample based on the responses of fifty employees.

marketing focus. However, the majority of employees accepted that it was part of their job, and because the bank was changing they too would have to change with it. Some of the more recent recruits knew no different, as the sales orientation was in place when they joined. Adapting to a new consumer focus was therefore not so much of a problem. This was also a consequence of a change in Northbank's recruitment strategy which, according to the Area Personnel Manager, had been restructured to favour candidates with strong leadership and interpersonal skills, now considered crucial in promoting Northbank's services.

The amount of marketing and promotional activities in which employees could be expected to engage was highly dependent on the amount of time they were free to devote to the activity. This aspect more than any other reflected the status of marketing at Northbank. Employees were asked to indicate the amount of time they spent on marketing. Half of the sample indicated that they spent between 5–25 per cent of their time on marketing related activities. Only 10 per cent of employees indicated that they spent more than half their time on marketing activities (see Table 4.3). These findings suggest that although Northbank has moved some way towards a marketing orientation, this was by no means a thorough reorganisation. Many staff at Northbank commented that consumer-centred marketing was extremely time consuming, and they were unwilling to engage in the activity even when opportunities presented themselves (see also Howcroft 1992 on this point). Most employees believed that operational tasks should be given priority, while marketing was an optional extra. It was clear that Northbank's employees would need to spend a greater proportion of their time selling services in the future if the bank was to continue its quest to be a financial retailer.

The policy of making all employees part-time marketeers also caused a degree of conflict among managers who had responsibility for different functions. The specialisation among the management structure between

*Table 4.3* Analysis of time Northbank's employees spent on marketing activities

| % of time | Grade of employee | | | | | Total % |
|---|---|---|---|---|---|---|
| | 2 | 3 | 4 | 5 | Managerial | |
| Less than 5% | 2 | 6 | 2 | 2 | 2 | 14 |
| 5–25% | 2 | 20 | 12 | 6 | 10 | 50 |
| 25–50% | 2 | 8 | 10 | 4 | 2 | 26 |
| 50%+ | – | – | 4 | 4 | 2 | 10 |
| Total | 6 | 34 | 28 | 16 | 16 | 100 |

*Source:* Burton (1992); sample based on the responses of fifty employees.

branch, lending and operations managers meant that to some extent managers were all pulling in different directions in order to meet their own targets. Branch managers were under pressure to achieve their branch's marketing targets and wanted staff to a give priority to personal selling. Operations managers, on the other hand, were responsible for the branches' administrative functions and data processing. Operations managers placed most emphasis on increasing the effectiveness of the throughput of work in the branches. In many ways the increase in efficiency and productivity of administrative tasks was incompatible with spending time selling financial services to customers at every opportunity that presented itself. It was theoretically appealing and, on the face of it, cost effective to attempt to change the organisation's culture by using the part-time marketeer strategy to make marketing everybody's business. However, it is not clear how effective this policy is in practice.

An important ingredient which the part-time marketeer strategy neglected was employees' own commitment to marketing activity. Exploring the concept of internal marketing is useful in this regard (Berry and Parasuraman 1991; Gronroos 1984). The concept of internal marketing starts with the assumption that the quality of employees affects the overall quality of the service because of the labour intensive nature of most service provision. In order for organisations to promote marketing successfully, they must first engage in internal marketing. According to Berry and Parasuraman, 'Internal marketing is attracting, developing, motivating and retaining qualified employees through job-products that satisfy their needs. Internal marketing is the philosophy of treating employees as customers' (1991: 151). The internal marketing concept draws attention to the view that before service employees can market an organisation's products effectively, the employment-related needs of staff should be satisfied.

It is not clear that the competitive environment in which financial service organisations are operating in Britain is conducive to extensive internal marketing. Not unlike many other financial organisations in the late 1980s and early 1990s, Northbank had embarked on a substantial project of branch closure and job cuts in an attempt to reduce its cost:income ratio. Northbank employees were very conscious of this, and morale among clerical workers was low. The recession-hit early 1990s was a stark contrast to the boom era of the early 1980s, when financial institutions had been concerned that they would be unable to recruit enough staff because of the demographic decline in school leavers (Salway 1989). Northbank's internal reorganisation, which had transformed some branches to hi-tech money shops, had the effect of reducing the number of managerial posts. This contributed to a stagnant internal labour market which provided employees with little prospect of promotion. Employees, both clerical and managerial, expressed real concern about the lack of promotion prospects in the forseeable future. This was a disappointment for many employees who had anticipated that, on joining the bank, they would have a career rather than 'just a job'. The practice within many financial institutions of recruiting management trainees, rather than exclusively promoting staff internally to management positions, intensified this situation (Rajan 1987b; Crompton and Sanderson 1990). Most employees resigned themselves to the fact that their promotion prospects looked bleak. Other negative changes included longer working hours and Saturday opening. A number of Northbank's employees openly admitted that they were looking for other jobs. The Area Personnel Manager was acutely aware that staff morale was low. Had local labour markets in the area not been so depressed, he suggested that more employees would have left. However, it is not just the banking industry which has suffered from significant levels of discontent among its employees. The turnover of direct sales staff in the insurance industry is a case in point. Some companies have a turnover of staff in excess of 50 per cent in their first year, and up to 90 per cent in their second year (Wiesner 1992).

It appeared that Northbank had important problems to resolve in its attempts to persuade employees to become more active in cross-selling financial products. According to one manager 'the stick was in more evidence than the carrot'. This position tended to be reinforced by the next issue to be discussed, that of performance related pay.

## BUCKS FOR BEHAVIOUR: THE RISE OF PERFORMANCE RELATED REMUNERATION IN THE FINANCIAL SERVICES SECTOR

Management control in service industries is difficult to operationalise because of the nature of the service delivery. Services are often intangible and consist of a process rather than a product. In the case of manufactured products, detailed specifications can be planned in advance and quality control can be tested beforehand. However, because of the nature of the service transaction, where consumption and production usually occur simultaneously, the difficulty of standardising the service delivery becomes more problematic. The aim of management is to ensure that a specific standard of behaviour is adopted by all employees, without it appearing false and enforced. Because managers are unable to survey every single transaction between consumers and staff, financial service employees have a degree of autonomy in their interaction with consumers. In Fox's (1985) terminology, many employees in the financial services sector are engaged in a 'high trust' employee/employer relationship. This situation necessitates a substantial element of self-control and discretion on the part of employees. Marshall (1985: 39) has indicated that service firms with 'a strong 'service ethic' will increase the discretionary effort of its employees'.

A range of novel ways have been designed by organisations to uncover poor service quality, and whether or not employees are relating to customers in ways viewed as desirable by their employers. These include strategies such as telephone surveys, focus groups, pretend shoppers, and a systematic analysis of letters of complaint. Systems of control such as these have led Fuller and Smith (1991: 11) to argue that moves towards a more consumer-orientated philosophy opens up the 'space' for consumer control, or management by consumers. As they state, 'consumers' reports broaden managerial power augumenting with it consumer power; conflicts between employers and employees may thus be reconstituted as conflicts between employees and consumers'. Another strategy used by management to encourage the commitment from employees has been the introduction performance related remuneration.

Payment for performance, or 'bucks for behaviour' as Kanter (1987) would have it, is not new; it is a practice as old as employment itself. However, there does appear to have been a marked increase in the use of various forms of pay flexibility in Britain in the 1980s (Atkinson 1984). An ACAS (1988) survey of 584 workplaces undertaken in 1987 revealed that 26 per cent of the sample had introduced profit sharing and 24 per cent had introduced merit pay in the previous three years. There has also been a noticeable trend in extending performance related pay initiatives to employees who have traditionally not been covered. Otley (1991) has noted that it was not unusual for senior managers at board level to receive profit related bonuses or to participate in share option schemes. Similarly, production workers have traditionally received bonuses for meeting production targets, or have been paid on a piecework basis.

However, a significant trend since the mid-1980s has been an increase in performance related pay for middle managers. In 1989 it was estimated that approximately 40 per cent of middle managers in the UK were receiving monetary payments for the attainment of performance targets. Previously, middle managers received a fixed salary without the inclusion of performance related pay, often not even receiving payments for overtime.

Employees in the insurance industry have traditionally been paid on the basis of commission on sales or premiums, plus a low basic salary. Likewise, profit sharing schemes and merit pay have been utilised in banking for some considerable length of time. However, more recently the financial services sector has been at the forefront of pay flexibility in an attempt to promote a more market-led orientation. The Banking Insurance and Finance Union (BIFU) has suggested that the recent upsurge in the use of performance related pay in the financial sector has a number of different causes. First, performance related remuneration is one way in which financial organisations can motivate individuals to identify with corporate goals and to associate their performance with that of the organisation. Second, performance related pay has been used to foster an internal culture of competition, mirroring that faced by financial service organisations in the marketplace. BIFU's main concern about performance related pay initiatives relates to the fact that they are supposedly based on 'objective' and 'scientific' targets. However, they are often neither objective nor scientific, and do not take into account the internal organisation of the workplace. Performance related pay systems also tend to reward output, and do not take into account the effort individuals put into their work (BIFU 1988).

Like many other financial service organisations in the 1980s, Northbank devised an elaborate performance related pay initiative. Two systems were introduced, one for management and another for clerical employees. All managers at Northbank were subject to performance related pay which was linked to a range of predetermined annual objectives. The successful achievement of targets was crucial for managers. It was a generally held view that their salary, bonus, career progression, status and, at the end of the day, job security all revolved around their marketing expertise and the meeting of targets. This is a similar situation to that documented in the insurance industry by Knights and Morgan (1990), where the achievement of targets held important implications for an individual's identity within an organisation. They state, 'Failing to achieve a target is not just a matter of suffering economic and political sanctions, it also threatens the sense of a manager's or a sales person's subjective competence' (1990: 373).

Managerial objectives at Northbank took the form of qualitative and qualitative targets. Quantitative, volumetric targets required branch managers to attain a year on increase in 17 different services. Qualitative targets and monitoring focused on business retention and the credit worthiness of customer loans. Utilisation of facilities, return on capital and increased income levels were cited as examples of others. Branch managers were also targeted on cost control, such as keeping paid overtime to a minimum. All managers were also responsible for providing 'leads' (customers who might be a good prospect for insurance, a pension or other investment) to the bank's personal investment financial advisors.

The targeting processes in operation at Northbank did cause a degree of resentment among managers on a number of different levels. First, the view was expressed that the targets managers had to obtain were presented as objectives whereas, in reality they were imposed. Managers felt that they should have been consulted more, especially as targets were linked directly to their salary. Second, in a number of cases managers received their annual objectives some way into the year – half way through in one case. This situation was viewed as unacceptable by many managers, who considered that the scheme should have been organised more professionally. Third, the way in which objectives were allocated appeared highly subjective and took relatively little account of the economic profile of consumers in their area. Fourth, as far as attaining volumetric targets was concerned, a lot of emphasis was given to increasing the quantity of business. There was much less emphasis on monitoring qualitative issues such as profitability; for example, whether the financial services being sold were being sold for the right reasons, whether they were being used by consumers and if they were being used in a way which was profitable for the bank. Obviously high sales volumes do not necessarily equate with high income generation (Shapiro *et al.* 1987). On a similar issue, a substantial number of managers felt that overenthusiastic target setting had fostered a culture of short termism and not one of long-term profitability. Finally, the setting of objectives had the effect of demoralising some managers. Managerial objectives were set at such a high level that only one branch manager out of a total of twenty-two had achieved all his targets.

While managerial employees received monetary benefits for

achieving personal targets, clerical employees were offered prizes for the achievement of branch targets. Northbank was not alone in providing non-cash incentives – they have recently become an important way of rewarding and motivating employees in a number of industries in Britain (*Personnel Management* 1992). However, the choice of prizes rather than cash kept Northbank on the right side of BIFU, who did not approve of performance related pay for clerical employees. The theory behind the 'points make prizes' concept was formulated by the bank in the hope of encouraging dependable behaviour of a consistently acceptable standard and securing high commitment and effort among clerical employees. The object of the exercise was to convert the successful attainment of branch targets into points, which were subsequently converted into prizes. Prizes were then chosen from a catalogue at the end of the year (see Burton 1991 for more details). According to exponents of expectancy theory (see Porter and Lawler 1968), an employee's decision of how much effort to expend on a particular task will be highly dependent on how much they value the outcome. However, the rewards structure of the scheme at Northbank bore no relationship to individual effort whatsoever. Regardless of who sold the various services, all clerical employees within a branch were awarded the same number of points for achieving specific volumetric targets. In practice, the opportunity employees had to sell bank products was highly dependent on the location they occupied in the occupational structure. While some employees had a very marketing-oriented role, for example customer counsellor, others, particularly in the larger administrative branches, did not hold such positions. This situation gave rise to the view that too much pressure was being put on a relatively small number of employees to achieve branch targets. A league table was displayed in all branches which kept staff up-to-date on how many products had been sold and how their branch compared with others. However, in one of the branches, the manager kept a league table showing which staff sold which services and periodically gave the top salesperson a cash bonus. This gesture caused a great deal of resentment among clerical employees.

## CONCLUSION

In the absence of extensive price and product competition, financial institutions have fostered and encouraged service quality as an important competitive strategy. A number of human resource policies have been implemented to support this change in organisational culture. They have included acknowledging the importance of interpersonal and communication skills, relative to technical skills, by placing experienced personnel in problem resolution positions. Incorporating customer care into mainstream employment training and instigating quality circles were other examples. In an attempt to ensure that customers' needs are fulfilled in-house, employees were encouraged to engage in person-centred marketing. However, the results at Northbank indicated that the transition from administration to marketing tasks was not straightforward. The main barrier to 'relationship banking' was the lack of time which could be committed to the activity. While most employees considered marketing an important part of their job, in practice operational tasks came first. Northbank had replaced older style managers with those who had more marketing awareness and were prepared to actively market the bank's services. While it had been possible to remove most managers from their post by offering early retirement, the same could not be attempted with clerical staff because of the shear weight of numbers involved. Many of Northbank's clerical employees had been recruited during a previous era, when good administrators rather than articulate sellers were required. It was clear that not all of them had made the transition. Finally, the financial service sector was at the forefront of the introduction of pay flexibility in the 1980s in the hope that it would encourage further marketing activity among staff. However, the case study at Northbank indicated that while schemes had been introduced, their practical application left a lot to be desired.

## SUMMARY

**Service quality became an important competitive tool in the financial services sector in the 1980s and 1990s for two reasons:**

1 **a lack of price and product competition;**
2 **and the considerable benefits of total quality management strategies in relation to both financial savings and positive consumer perceptions.**

**Service quality strategies also had important implications for human resource management policies including:**

1 **the heightened importance of interpersonal and marketing skills within the workforce;**
2 **the implementation of training schemes, including quality circles, which focused on customer care and marketing;**
3 **and the introduction of performance related remuneration.**

# Chapter 5

# Consumer financial behaviour

In the past, when the consumption of financial services was limited to a select minority of the population, consumer behaviour was fairly predictable. One of the features of the 1980s and 1990s has been the increasing unpredictability of consumers' financial behaviour. This change has two main sources. The first is that financial service users have become a heterogeneous group in relation to both their social and economic characteristics (see Chapter 2). The days when financial service consumers were mainly comprised of the affluent, well-educated middle classes have disappeared. The complex structure of contemporary financial service consumers has made it difficult for producers to determine how different groups of consumers will behave. Second, contemporary financial service consumers are no longer dependent on the advice and guidance of producers when making their purchase decisions. Financial service advice has been popularised by the media through newspapers, magazines, radio and television. Virtually every daily newspaper has a personal finance section which advises on money matters. The interest in financial services has even spread to the tabloids. For example, the *Sun* has been running a financial section since 1987 (Folly 1990). Likewise, the Consumers' Association publishes a financial section through its *Which?* magazine, highlighting the pros and cons of various financial service products. The informal learning opportunities afforded to financial service consumers have expanded rapidly since the beginning of the 1980s.

In this chapter, it will be argued that the variability of consumer behaviour in the 1980s and 1990s has meant that financial institutions have been unable to predict the consumption of financial services with the same degree of accuracy as has previously been the case. The unpredictability of consumer behaviour has been demonstrated in a number of ways. The days have gone when generations of the same family would use the same financial service institution throughout their lifetimes. Consumers are becoming more selective about the types of financial institutions they deal with, and a growing number have spread their financial affairs among a number of providers. Financial institutions have also learnt that changing consumer behaviour can be a lengthy process. Even in instances where financial services have been accepted and used by consumers, this has not always been in the manner anticipated by financial institutions. From the 1970s onwards, financial institutions fashioned and promoted a whole range of money transmission systems in an attempt to reduce the labour intensive nature of many areas of financial service work. Unfortunately, consumer attitudes to and acceptance of some of these initiatives has been variable. As consumers have become more financially astute, they have found ways of 'playing the system' which have brought them into conflict with producers. This issue will be illustrated by the clashes over the 'correct' use of credit cards which occurred in the late 1980s.

Financial service institutions have spent enormous amounts of money on branch refurbishment programmes to make them more consumer friendly. However, recent research findings suggest that this strategy has not been particularly effective, and that consumers avoid going into branches whenever possible. The issue of independent advice in relation to purchasing investment products was given a high profile in the 1986 Financial Services Act. It was thought that consumers would wish to use independent advisers for advice about a range of different services on the market. However, many consumers wish to make purchase decisions on the basis of information from informal sources, and this has led to a number of producers re-thinking their strategy. The final area of discussion focuses on deviant behaviour in the form of fraud. This is a feature of consumer behaviour which is increasing rapidly in Britain, and is certainly one which producers find difficult to predict.

The first issue to be discussed relates to the rate at which consumers change their financial service provider, given that this has traditionally been an important measure of customer loyalty.

## CONSUMERS ON THE MOVE

Deregulation of the financial markets has enabled consumers to pick and choose from a wide range of different financial service suppliers. This has often led to the view that consumers have become more discriminating and reflexive. However, this is an assertion which is more often made than proved. Because more products and suppliers are available, it does not necessarily follow that consumers will 'shop around'. Nevertheless, there does appear to be growing evidence that some consumers are becoming less loyal to financial institutions. One of the most influential measures of consumer behaviour in personal financial services is the number of consumers who change financial institutions. A recent National Opinion Poll (NOP)/Financial Research Service Findings report (cited in Thomson 1992c) indicated that consumers are increasingly footloose. The research indicated that between 2–4 per cent of consumers close their current account each year. However, industry estimates are frequently higher than those cited in the NOP survey. In 1986, it was estimated that an annual figure of between 4–10 per cent of customers changed their financial service institution (Thomson 1986). A more revealing finding from the NOP survey was that 46 per cent of all bank current accounts opened were the result of transfers. An all-time high figure of 600,000 consumers chose to transfer their account to another institution. There are obviously a range of reasons, moving house, changing job, getting divorced, and so on, which might cause consumers to re-evaluate their relationship with financial institutions. Nevertheless, the findings have demonstrated that customer inertia, which at one time might have prevented consumers from moving their business elsewhere, is being eroded. Undoubtedly, changing one's current account to another provider is not a straightforward process, especially if standing orders, direct debits and salaries are paid in and out of the account. Many bankers had thought that the associated disruption and hassle this process would cause might dissueade those consumers contemplating a move (Nevans 1987). For significant numbers of consumers in Britain, this does not appear to be the case any longer. A similar trend of consumers shopping around for the best deal has also become apparent in the insurance industry. In 1993, consumers were more than twice as likely to switch their household and car insurance policies to another financial institution as they were 18 months previously (Meller 1993).

Another important indicator of customer loyalty has been the number of consumers who have accounts at more than one financial institution. The trend towards dual or second account holding is on the increase in Britain, and it provides an opportunity for consumers to play one financial institution off against another. In 1986 15 per cent of consumers had accounts at more than one bank, an increase of 40 per cent on the previous twelve months. However, this figure is still lower than some other European countries. In France, dual account holding has been estimated to be as high as 25 per cent (Thomson 1986). Second account holding has heightened the degree of competition between those banks and building societies which directly compete for customers. Research by the Association for Payment Clearing Services (1989) (APACS) has suggested that well over half of the consumers who open building society accounts also have a current account with a bank. Young people are particularly inclined to have accounts at more than one financial institution. Lewis and Bingham's (1991) research of 16–24-year-olds in the Manchester area indicated that nearly a quarter of young people had an account at more than one bank. A range of reasons were given, including locational convenience, a greater choice of services, more cash points, the availability of more money and free gifts. The NOP findings also indicated that there was a regional dimension to second account holding. The highest figure, 17 per cent, was in the south of England, compared with 9 per cent in Scotland and the north of England (cited in Thomson 1992c).

Multi-holding of plastic cards is also a feature of contemporary consumer behaviour in Britain. In 1988, only 15 per cent of card holders had three or more cards, while 60 per cent had only one. By 1991, 27 per cent of consumers had three or more cards, while 44 per cent had only one. These figures indicate a sharp increase in multiple card holding between 1988 and 1991. Showing a similar pattern to that observed in account holding, multiple card holding was most frequently found among middle-aged groups of consumers, and those in the AB socio-economic groups (the two highest social groups). Around 50 per cent of ABs who possessed cards had at least three (APACS 1992).

In the past, only middle-aged individuals in the higher socio-economic groups tended to switch financial institutions; now the 'younger and less well healed are on the move' (Thomson 1992a: 6). The under-25-year-old age group has been particularly willing to close and move account. In 1991, 45 per cent of NatWest's customers who closed their accounts were under 25. This finding was also supported by Lewis and Bingham's (1991) research, which found that 28 per cent of respondents had already changed a bank or building society account. University students demonstrated the greatest tendency to switch, at 36 per cent. Similar trends are also evident in the household insurance market. Consumers who switch provider tend to be younger and drawn from the higher socio-economic groups (Meller 1993). It tends to be the lower socio-economic groups that remain loyal to financial institutions. Jain et al. (1987: 66) have noted that 'the bank loyal segment was found to be relatively older, less educated, less affluent and concentrated in blue collar occupations. The loyal segment places much greater emphasis on the human aspects of banking while the non-loyal segment is swayed by economic rationale.' This feature of consumer behaviour is particularly advan-tageous to banks such as the Trustee Savings Bank, the Co-op Bank, and many building societies who have large numbers of consumers drawn from the lower socio-economic groups. How long this apparent loyalty will last is debatable. It was not so long ago that switching from one financial service firm to another was unheard of, as was the increasing trend of holding an account at more than one institution. Trends in the motor insurance market suggest that customer loyalty among consumers in the lower socio-economic groups may already be declining. Recent research suggests that consumers who tend to switch provider most frequently are the very young and those from blue collar, manual occupations (Meller 1993).

There is growing evidence to indicate that consumers are willing to change supplier and use more than one provider to meet their financial needs. This practice is at odds with the strategies adopted by many financial institutions to market themselves as one-stop financial supermarkets, providing a wide range of services. A number of consumers in the higher socio-economic categories and younger age groups have decided to spread their financial business among a number of providers. However, while consumers have been willing to change financial service provider, they have often demonstrated a resistance to accepting new products and processes. The next section highlights the ways in which consumers have demonstrated a reluctance to change their behaviour, despite initiatives by producers to persuade them to do so.

## THE CASHLESS SOCIETY: MYTH OR REALITY?

During the 1970s a cashless society was thought to be not far from reality for advanced industrial economies. This prediction particularly appealed to financial institutions because the handling of cash is a labour intensive and costly activity. Most financial institutions have introduced a variety of money transmission systems, such as cheques, ATMs, electronic funds transfer at the point of sale (EFTPOS), and home and telephone banking, to reduce the labour intensive nature of financial service work. However, despite the great variation in money transmission systems introduced in advanced, industrial societies, they have one feature in common – the continued dominance of cash as the most important medium of exchange. The real value of cash in circulation in European countries did not decline significantly in the 1980s.

In Britain the use of cash as the predominant medium of exchange has changed little since the mid-1970s (see Table 5.1). While the introduction

*Table 5.1* How payments are made

|        | Cash | Cheque | Standing order/ direct debit | Other |
|--------|------|--------|------------------------------|-------|
|        | %    | %      | %                            | %     |
| 1976*  | 93   | 4      | 2                            | 1     |
| 1981   | 88   | 6.5    | 3                            | 2.5   |
| 1984   | 86   | 6.5    | 4                            | 3.5   |
| 1989   | 78   | 12     | 4.5                          | 5.5   |

*Source:* APACS (1989).
*Note:* * 50p or more; all other years £1 or more.

of some automated payment systems has reduced the overall volume of cash transactions, for example electronic funds transfer at the point of sale (EFTPOS) and credit cards, others, especially the use of automatic teller machines (ATMs), have increased the use of cash. The imposition of transaction charges may also have contributed to the buoyant volume of cash payments. Financial institutions are in the contradictory position of reinforcing cash as a medium of exchange under some circumstances and doing the exact opposite in others. However, widespread customer acceptance of new innovations can be as problematic as a low take-up rate. This issue has been illustrated in Britain in relation to ATMs. In recent years the use of ATMs has witnessed a dramatic increase, especially among consumers in the under 30 age group (Inter-Bank Research Organisation 1985). Among current account holders in Britain, the percentage of instances where ATMs have been used to access cash increased from 7 per cent in 1981 to 32 per cent in 1991 (APACS 1992). However, one of the problems associated with this increase, from a financial service provider's point of view, is that while the value of cash withdrawals from ATMs has increased, so has the volume of transactions.

Data provided by APACS (1988) has indicated that the volume of ATM withdrawals appears to be approximately twice that of cheque encashment for the same value. In terms of the average withdrawal per ATM visit worldwide, the Swiss had the highest average with CHF 335 (£127), the lowest being Portugal with £33. The UK and the Republic of Ireland were the second lowest with an average withdrawal of £39 (Battelle Institute 1989; Financial Times 1989). In terms of cost effectiveness, the widely quoted break even levels of 4,000 withdrawals per machine per month are not being reached by some financial organisations, given that the UK average is 5,100 withdrawals per ATM a month (Battelle Institute 1989). Unexpected consumer behaviour of this nature has meant that ATM costs have remained relatively high. Some of the banks have tried to combat this trend by increasing the minimum value of a withdrawal from £5 to either £10 or £20.

The facility of automated payments such as direct debits has been around for some twenty years. However, there are still relatively few consumers who use this payment method. At the end of the 1980s 92.5 per cent of consumers did not even use automated payments to pay their gas bills. Research has indicated that consumers believe the use of automated payments reduces their control over their account, and this has prevented a more extensive take-up. An area which BACS (formerly the Bankers' Automated Clearing Service) considered had future potential was the automated payment of the community charge, to which end a £2.6 million nationwide television campaign was launched (*Marketing* 1989). The subsequent withdrawal of the community charge system has meant that much of the planning and advertising will have to be repeated.

It is expected that automated payments will become more popular among consumers because of a number of factors. The first is the automation of many government payments, for example child benefit and pensions. State benefits alone account for over one billion payments annually, the vast majority being cashed at post offices. However, there may be a reluctance to use automated payments by those who need immediate cash and by others who do not possess a current account. The second factor is the automated payment of salaries, discussed already in Chapter 2. While the attitude of weekly-paid workers to automated payments has been conservative, banks have also been reluctant to promote weekly payments because of the high operating costs involved. This situation will probably change in the future.

One habit which consumers have been reluctant to give up is writing cheques. British financial service consumers' commitment to cheques as a preferred method of payment is a long standing characteristic. In 1992 a little over 2.5 million cheques were written in Britain, compared with 2 million in 1982 (British Bankers' Association 1993). Despite the moves by financial institutions and retailers towards payment by plastic, the cheque is still considered the ever-enduring 'dinosaur' of the payments industry (Penn 1991). The favouritism accorded to cheques by consumers has manifested itself in recent years by the pressure for higher value cheque guarantee cards. Since 1977 it has been standard practice for banks to issue cheque cards to a value of £50, an increase of £20 on the original figure. More recently, retailers and consumer organisations have rallied for an increase in cheque card limits in line with the rate of inflation; a figure of £125 has been cited as more realistic. Cheque cards with a value of £100 were introduced by most of the clearing banks for particular groups of customers, usually those with above average incomes, as a response to pressure from retailers. However, consumers have been reticent in applying for the higher value card. By the end of 1990, only 10 per cent of cheque cards issued were for limits in excess of £50 (Penn 1991).

It is clearly important for producers to monitor the ways in which consumers use their financial service products to ensure that the profitability of different areas of business can be evaluated. It was just this process of evaluation that caused considerable consumer–producer conflict in the late 1980s over the 'correct' use of credit cards. The next section considers this issue in more detail.

## CONSUMERS, CONFLICT AND CREDIT CARDS

The credit card industry is one which has expanded rapidly, not only in Britain, but worldwide. In the late 1980s Visa was expanding at a massive rate of 52 per cent a year (Kosciusko 1989). The number of credit cards issued in Britain has been enormous since the first credit card, Barclaycard, was launched in 1966. In the decade 1980–90 the number of Mastercards increased by 265 per cent, and Visa by 149 per cent. In 1992, the total number of Mastercard and Visa cards issued in Britain was 26.5 million (British Bankers' Association 1992). By the end of the 1980s, some of the largest retailers in Britain had a combined total of 10 million store credit card accounts (Bliss 1988). Consumers have tended to use credit cards for large value payments. This feature is reflected in the purchases for which credit cards are most frequently used: paying for petrol, holidays, and at supermarkets (Ellwood 1989; Worthington 1992).

While financial service institutions have profited from the credit card boom, they have not always identified and conceptualised consumer behaviour accurately. Towards the end of the 1980s, the issue of how credit cards should be used was the subject of intense conflict between some financial service producers and their consumers. As consumers have become better informed, they have acquired an awareness of 'how to play the system' to their advantage. In the case of credit cards, this was manifest in consumers using credit cards as a convenient method of payment, as an interest free overdraft, by paying their bill in full at the end of each month. On average, 45 per cent of consumers settled their account at the end of each month, while most other credit card holders settled within 2–3 months. This practice was at odds with how financial institutions intended the cards to be used, that is for the purpose of obtaining credit in exchange for the payment of interest.

The practice of using credit cards as a source of interest free credit prompted Lloyds to charge its three million Access card holders a fee of £12 per annum from 1 February 1990 in return for lower interest rates on outstanding balances. Lloyds conceded that 37 per cent of its Access holders who paid their bill in full each month, and therefore paid no interest, would gain no benefit. Initially, the move to charge a fee lost Lloyds around 15 per cent of its credit card customers. The credit card Director of Save and Prosper, a company which offered a lower interest rate than both Visa and Mastercard and did not charge an annual fee, estimated that they were receiving approximately 400 applications per day from Lloyds Bank Access holders. He stated that in many cases applicants were professionals, with above-average incomes and with a relationship with Lloyds stretching back 15–25 years. Lloyds was the first British bank to charge consumers an annual fee for the use of its credit card. However, this move was shortly followed by Barclays, who charged its 9 million Barclaycard holders an annual fee of £8 from mid-June 1990, and by Midland who charged a fee of £10 from April 1991 (Financial Times 1990a, 1990b). The net result of the revised 'rules' over the use of credit cards was that consumers voted with their feet. They cut up and then sent back their credit cards to the issuers in their thousands. This example has also illustrated that consumers have become more discriminating and reflexive, and they have made their position on specific issues known to financial institutions. However, the example does reveal that financial service producers still have an enormous amount of power which they can deploy against the consumer. In this instance it was a case of financial institutions moving the goal posts.

Another area of consumer behaviour which has developed apace, but which producers can do little about, is the abandonment of high street branches. In Chapter 3, a range of initiatives were outlined which indicated that financial institutions were investing considerable resources in transforming their branch premises and installing relational databases to increase the marketing potential of their high street premises. However, it not clear how many consumers wish to avail themselves of the opportunity to visit high street branches. Some of the issues associated with the lack of customer contact will be discussed further in the following section.

## CUSTOMERS ABANDON HIGH STREET BRANCHES

The ways in which financial services can be delivered have undergone a series of rapid and profound changes. In the last ten years, developments in information technology have offered consumers numerous ways in which financial services can be delivered. This range has, to some extent, undermined the location of branches. The increasing number of ways in which the same or a similar service can be provided has made the consumption of financial services spatially indifferent. This is a characteristic which is not confined to Britain, but is also evident in other OECD countries (OECD 1989).

Throughout the 1980s financial institutions invested considerable financial resources in making their premises more user friendly. Refurbishment programmes were based on the assumption that consumers visiting branches are key marketing targets. However, recent research has suggested that consumers are visiting their branches relatively infrequently. Research conducted on behalf of Midland Bank (Mayers 1991) revealed that 20 per cent of consumers had not visited their branch in the last month, and 10 per cent had not visited their branch in the previous six months. Over half of the consumers questioned indicated that they would like to visit their branch as little as possible. With regards to the degree of customer contact between customers and staff, the research indicated that one-third of customers did not speak to any branch staff during their last visit. A significant proportion of customers preferred to make withdrawals from ATMs rather than over the bank counter. One explanation of the success of ATMs is that financial institutions have overcome consumer reluctance to use self-service technology. An alternative interpretation has been provided by Laurie (1989: 13), who has suggested that 'customers were only too glad to escape the branches' dark menacing interiors, even if it meant standing in the pouring rain, with a fistful of soggy fivers, looking tantalisingly appealing to any passing mugger'!

The lack of contact consumers have had with their local bank or building society branch has undermined the very function of refurbishment programmes aimed at facilitating person-to-person marketing. This has meant that financial institutions have missed important cross-selling opportunities. This scenario has prompted many financial institutions to consider other ways in which they might promote their products. An activity which has been earmarked to increase significantly in the near future is the use of direct mail. Research conducted by Ennew and Wright (1990) indicated that banks and building societies intended to make much more use of direct mail as a marketing channel in the 1990s.

Changing consumer behaviour has, nevertheless, provided new opportunities for financial institutions, especially in the areas of home, office and telephone banking. The most outstanding tele-banking scheme in Britain is Midland's First Direct. Launched on 1 October 1989 in a blaze of multimedia advertising costing around £6 million, First Direct is a person-to-person banking service operating twenty-four hours a day, 365 days of the year. Its head office consists of fifty staff employed in the City, while its 250 operations staff are located on the outskirts of Leeds. The service is primarily, although not exclusively, targeted at high income office workers who rarely visit a bank branch and are used to conducting business over the phone. By mid-1992 First Direct had signed up 200,000 customers; by the end of 1993 it expected 450,000. Approximately 85 per cent of First Direct's customers are from social categories A and B, comprising professionals and managers (Benady 1993). If the practice of banking by post, telephone and computer were to be embraced by large numbers of customers, it would present an excellent opportunity for competing organisations, possibly from Europe, to gain a foothold in the personal financial services sector market. Until recently, the main competitive barrier has been the existence of an extensive network of branches which has proved too costly for competitors to build up from scratch (Whelan 1989).

Another area where consumer behaviour has proved unpredictable has been the issue of independent advice. The 1986 Financial Services Act placed a great emphasis on improving the quality of advice and information given by financial service organisations to consumers. However, it is becoming increasingly clear that large numbers of consumers have little interest in accessing independent advice from financial service firms, but would rather gain the necessary market intelligence through other channels. The issue of independent advice is discussed further in the following section.

## CUSTOMER ACCEPTANCE OF INDEPENDENT ADVICE

One of the most important changes following the 1986 Financial Services Act was the concept of polarisation as it applied to the promotion of financial service investment and savings products. Financial organisations were compelled by the terms of the Act to choose between offering products as agents or providing independent advice. Under the Act financial advisers had to sell either the best investment products from the whole marketplace or solely the products of one company for which they acted as agents. One of the main functions of the Act was to bring out into the open the often complex relationship between financial service companies and their agents and intermediaries. The Act therefore enabled consumers to make the choice between a product from a known, reputable producer or the best deal from all the products on the market.

Shortly after the Act was introduced it became clear that most financial organisations had adopted the tied agent route. In 1989, among the largest four clearing banks and top ten building societies, only NatWest and three building societies had chosen the 'independent' category. By 1992 none of the largest banks provided independent advice. Shelton (1990) has indicated that in 1987, 60 per cent of investment business was purchased through the 'independent' route, as opposed to an estimated figure of 37 per cent after the introduction of the Financial Services Act. It appeared that financial institutions had assessed the financial costs of providing advice and guidance and co-ordinating operations between different financial institutions, and chose to earn the best commissions from insurance companies rather than seek out the best deal for consumers. The strategies adopted by financial institutions might be perceived as providing consumers with less choice than the Act had originally intended. However, recent research has demonstrated that receiving independent advice has not been given a high priority among many consumers.

Ennew's (1992) research into 140 consumers in the East Midlands found that, while 60 per cent of her sample understood the function of independent advisors, not all sought their advice. The results indicated that the more consumers read the financial pages of newspapers and listened to finance related programmes on television and radio, the less likely they were to use independent financial advisors. What was somewhat surprising, given the finding above, was that independent financial advisors were favoured by the higher economic social groups. Ennew attributed the use of independent financial advisors by the higher social groups as a function of their lifestyles. Particularly important in this regard could be the lack of time busy professionals are able to devote to financial service intelligence gathering. The acquisition of independent financial advice was also sought by younger consumers. However, this finding could be attributed to younger consumers' lack of knowledge about financial service products rather than the lack of time to shop around. Factors such as trust, convenience, income, and knowledge of the Financial Services Act had little impact on the motivation of consumers to use independent financial advisors.

The issue of independent advice highlights, in part at least, the ability of consumers to affect the policies of some of the major financial institutions. Since it became apparent that many consumers did not value the acquisition of independent advice, more companies took the tied agent route. Nevertheless, it also needs to be recognised that many financial institutions chose to become agents before consumers had the opportunity to make their wishes felt.

The final issue to be discussed is deviant consumer behaviour. Soloman (1992) has defined deviant behaviour as anti-consumption. Both of these concepts are useful in the discussion of consumer behaviour in the financial services sector.

## DEVIANT CONSUMER BEHAVIOUR: THE CASE OF FRAUD

The 1980s will be remembered among the financial services community and consumers alike for the Bank of Credit and Commerce International (BCCI) scandal, dubbed the biggest fraud in banking history. However, consumer fraud is also on the increase. Fraud levels in the financial services industry are reaching epidemic proportions. Cheque card fraud nearly trebled between 1981 and 1990, up from £11.7 to £31.3 million. Similarly, in the early 1990s, plastic card fraud was the second largest category of theft after burglary. Fraud levels at Mastercard increased from £3.3 million in 1981 to £37.3 million in 1991. Loses at Visa were even higher, at £43.6 million in 1991 (British Bankers' Association 1992). However, fraud is not confined to plastic card transactions. Banks justified their reluctance to increase the value of cheque cards by using the fear of fraud. Around 100,000 cheque cards are lost or stolen each year. When the limit was raised from £30 to £50 in 1977, fraud rose by 98 per cent the following year (*Guardian* 1989).

Anti-fraud campaigns via advertisements in newspapers, on public hoardings and direct approaches to retailers in the form of videos have helped to reduce the amount lost by the banks (APACS 1987). However, it is not only financial institutions which have sustained losses due to fraud, but also retailers. Indeed many retailers have turned to cheque guarantee companies to help them beat fraud. Transax, one of the biggest companies of this nature operating in the UK, oversees the authorisation of £55 million in transactions each month from a subscriber base of 32,000 outlets throughout the country. The service also covers business cheques which fall outside the scope of business guarantee cards. Transax operates from its own database; the clearing banks do not provide confidential information relating to their customers' accounts. If a cheque, accepted by a retailer within the scheme, is subsequently returned unpaid, the retailer keeps the amount in question, while the debt collecting division of Transax recovers the amount outstanding. The cheque guarantee company business is much more developed in the US, Australia and New Zealand, where banks subscribe to the firms themselves and use it before opening accounts as part of a credit assessment process (Penn 1991).

The main growth area for theft in the early 1990s was debit card fraud. Debit cards such as Switch and Connect were introduced by banks in the late 1980s to enable consumers to pay for goods and services at the point of sale. Debit card losses through fraud at the point-of-sale increased from £26 million in 1988 to £114 million in 1991, partly as a result of organised crime. Fraud is at its worst in the Greater London area and the south, where losses can be up to three times the amount in other parts of the country. Debit card fraud is also concentrated in particular areas of the retail sector. Food, household furnishing and petrol purchases experience significantly higher levels of fraud than the national average (Howes 1992).

Clearly, financial service fraud is an area of consumer behaviour which is highly unpredictable. It is an issue which shows most clearly the inability of producers to manipulate consumers to the point where their behaviour becomes predictable.

## CONCLUSION

Consumers appear to be becoming more discerning in relation to their choice of financial service provider and the ways in which they use their accounts. In 1991 a record number of consumers transferred their account, and dual account holding became more widespread, particularly among consumers in the higher socio-economic groups and younger consumers. As consumer behaviour is becoming increasingly unpredictable, it is more difficult for producers to anticipate how consumers are going to use their accounts. The case of credit cards highlighted the conflict which can occur between producers and consumers when consumers are able to use accounts which fulfil their needs, but in ways which are not profitable for financial service institutions. Similarly, deviant consumer behaviour is costing financial service institutions millions of pounds a year. Each new product introduced provides an additional opportunity for consumer fraud. A key challenge for financial institutions is to keep one step ahead and design products which are vandal proof.

This chapter has discussed how consumer behaviour has affected the ways in which producers have dealt with consumers. However, what has become increasingly significant in the 1980s and 1990s is the power and rights individual consumers have derived from the activities of consumer groups, regulatory change and financial service ombudsmen who have promoted the consumer's viewpoint. The next chapter will discuss some of these issues in more depth.

## SUMMARY

Consumer behaviour has become more difficult to predict. A number of factors have indicated this:

1 consumers are more likely to change their financial service provider, and dual account holding has increased;
2 despite the strategies employed by financial service institutions to encourage consumers to use automated payments, consumers have prefered to use cash;
3 consumers have found ways to use accounts and plastic cards which producers had not forseen;
4 refurbishment programmes to attract consumers into high street branches do have not appear to have been effective;
5 most consumers have not valued independent advice;
6 fraud has increased at epidemic proportions.

# Chapter 6

# Consumerism comes to financial services

Financial institutions have become more consumer-orientated in their attitudes towards consumers in the last fifteen years. To understand fully why this shift has occurred, the relationship between financial service producers and consumers needs to be situated within a wider social context. In the 1980s, the combined effects of regulatory change, industry-based Ombudsmen schemes and the activities of consumer movements promoted an environment which was more supportive of consumer interest than ever before. In this chapter, there will be an assessment of the effects of regulatory change, in particular the 1986 Financial Services Act, in promoting a higher degree of consumer protection. The development of Financial Service Ombudsmen schemes provided consumers with an important avenue of redress. Each of the four ombudsman schemes will be considered in relation to its membership, terms of reference and the extent to which each is used by consumers. Some of the activities undertaken by consumer groups, notably the Consumers' Association and the National Consumer Council, in promoting the consumer's point of view will also be outlined.

Recent discussions on the issue of the consumer, and consumer interest, have also had implications for the way in which financial institutions are conceptualised. No longer are they held in high esteem, as guardians of the nation's wealth. Increasingly, the social role played by financial institutions has been recognised. This has opened up the 'space' for a discussion of business ethics, social obligation and what the 'proper' role of financial service organisations should be in an advanced, industrial economy such as Britain. The first issue to be addressed focuses on different perspectives on consumerism, and how they can be applied to the financial services sector.

## PERSPECTIVES ON CONSUMERISM

Consumer movements can be traced back to the beginning of commerce and trade. The accuracy and standardisation of weights, measures and the purity of food are all instances where the consumer's knowledge was inevitably weaker than the manufacturer. During the last century and the early years of the twentieth century, consumers were relatively well-informed when making purchase decisions because goods and needs were simple by comparison with today's standards. Consumers who needed information would often turn to a merchant who was probably a trusted friend or a proprietor who had developed a reputation for reliable advice. Consumerism, defined by Aaker and Day (1974: xvii) as being concerned with 'protecting consumers from all organisations with which there is an exchange relationship', has frequently been considered a product of the post-1945 era. Swann (1979) has indicated that, after the Second World War, governments paid much greater attention to legislation and organisations which were concerned with the producer–consumer relationship. Bodies such as the International Labour Organisation (ILO), the Organisation for Economic Co-operation and Development (OECD) and the European Community (EC) have all endeavoured to promote the interests of consumers. The growth of many consumers' organisations and associations also occurred during this period, as did 'grass roots' protection such as the Citizens' Advice Bureaux.

According to Mitchell (1978) the post-war, affluent consumer was faced with a 'problem of choice'. He has identified three main reasons why this was the case. The first was a consequence of the availability of a wide variety of goods and services which had not previously been mass produced. These 'new' goods and services came within the budgets of many families for the first time. Shopping therefore ceased to be a minor pre-occupation for the masses, and became an activity which generated a need for consumer information. Second, technological innovation increased the availability of new products with which consumers were not familiar. This factor led to a need for product information which dealt with the technicalities of these products. Finally, the dearth of information available from manufacturers, and the decline in personal advice from retailers, meant that consumers needed a source of information which they could trust and use as a basis for their purchase decisions. Consumer organisations were developed to fill this 'gap' in consumer information, education and advice.

Traditionally, consumer organisations have tended to focus on concerns which have related to manufactured goods rather than services. This factor may account for the relatively recent interest in consumerism in the financial service sector. This is a pattern which is not just apparent in Britain, but is evident in many other Western societies. An OECD survey conducted in 1987–8, indicated that, prior to the mid-1980s, most consumer complaints had focused on the quality and pricing of goods. The shift to a service economy for many industrial societies had generated an increasing number of service-related complaints. The report demonstrated that the increase in complaints about financial and related services was particularly marked (OECD 1989b).

Whether consumer organisations are in fact necessary mediators between producers and consumers is a debatable issue. It could be argued that market forces provide and maintain competition between firms. Competition keeps prices down by putting pressure on profit margins and stimulating higher levels of productivity and technological innovation. All of these features could be regarded as being in the consumer's best interest because they reduce costs and extend choice. This assumption that unfettered market forces would provide automatic benefits for consumers was critically evaluated by the Review Committee on Banking Services Law (1990) (frequently referred to as the Jacks Committee). Their report concluded that increased levels of competition in the banking industry had not generated a corresponding increase in the standards of banking practice. Jack (1992: 7) argued that there was 'strong evidence that confidence and trust, which was at the heart of the banker–customer relationship, had been eroded'. This was evident because the bank manager had become a salesman rather than a trusted financial advisor, because breaches in confidentiality occurred whereby personal information was used for marketing purposes for companies within the same financial group and finally because a less patient attitude had taken over from the friendly paternalism associated with an era when bankers could be trusted to do the 'decent' thing.

An alternative view of the producer–consumer relationship rejects the proposition that market forces provide consumers with sufficient protection in all situations and argues that consumers need protection under some circumstances and not others. Holton (1974) has argued that market competition is usually sufficient to provide consumers with protection under three circumstances: where goods and services are purchased by consumers on a regular basis; where goods and services have quality and performance standards which are apparent before and after use; and where goods and services are subject to low levels of technological innovation relative to the frequency of purchase. It is significant that many financial services do not fit into Holton's categories. Many financial service investment products such as insurance policies, unit trusts and pension plans are not purchased on a regular basis. Quality and performance standards associated with financial services are notoriously difficult to assess, as Chapter 3 demonstrated. It is not clear how accessible the process of evaluating complex financial services has been for many consumers. Finally, the rate of technological innovation in the financial services sector has been extraordinary in recent years. According to Holton's analysis, market competition alone would not assure financial service consumers the protection they need.

A more radical assessment of consumer–producer relations has been expressed by Gorse (1978). She has placed much more emphasis on the conflictual nature of the relationship, and has argued that consumer movements will be needed until the following conditions disappear:

1 Economic and commercial decisions, nationally and in firms, are taken without regard for consumer interests;
2 It is possible for a potentially good product to be spoilt because it has not been designed for durability, or ease of use, or economy in use;
3 It is possible for a good product to be ruined by an almost complete lack of quality control or failure to design packaging appropriate to the particular product, so that it is damaged in distribution;
4 Servicing is slow and unsatisfactory;
5 Services fall short of users' expectations;
6 Suppliers of goods and services fail to give their customers enough information to make a real choice.

This conflict of interests between producers and consumers identified by Gorse has been acknowledged by Gronmo and Olander (1991) in relation to the financial services sector. They have argued that it is often in the interest of financial institutions to keep consumers' knowledge to a minimum. This particularly applies to charges and fees, whereas it is in the consumers' interest to acquire as much knowledge as possible. Similarly, Jack (1992) has suggested that bankers, as many other professionals, have been reluctant to share 'trade secrets' which may serve to demystify the banking process.

Some financial institutions, particularly in the US, have taken a different line by arguing that educated consumers make better consumers. Consumer education has often been perceived as a bridge between consumers and financial institutions. For over a decade American Express has worked with the federal government's Consumer Information Centre, and has published and distributed educational pamphlets. The company has also experimented with reaching new groups of consumers. One of the most recent innovations has been to offer consumer seminars in churches under the auspices of church education. This has proved to be an effective way of reaching people who have already come together as a group (Fernstrom 1989; Waldrop 1991). However, not all consumer education and information programmes have been so enthusiastically endorsed. Trebilcock (1991: 430) for instance, is 'intuitively sceptical about the value of general precept-oriented consumer education (brochures, classroom education) remote in time and particularity from actual consumer choices that individuals face, where harder-edged information is typically required'. He has suggested that a more rigorous evaluation is needed of the costs to and benefits for consumers of such programmes.

The degree of protection consumers need is a matter of considerable debate. What became apparent in the 1980s was that the tide of government opinion and policy reflected the view that financial service consumers did require additional protection. Financial regulation was a key theme of the 1980s and is an issue which is discussed further in the next section.

## FINANCIAL REGULATION IN BRITAIN SINCE 1980

Financial organisations are frequently the most extensively regulated set of institutions within modern, industrial societies. The main aim of financial regulation has been the prevention of market failures, and hence the protection of market investors. According to Llewellyn (1987), the result has been a tendency for regulation to be conservative and anti-competitive, which has not entirely been in the consumer's best interest. The term deregulation is one which has been extensively used to describe changes within the financial services sector in Britain. However, there is some dispute as to whether that is an accurate conceptualisation of recent events. Mitchell (1992a) has argued that the term deregulation needs to be distinguished from 'unregulation'. He believes that the boundaries within and between financial institutions have been changed rather than abolished. Llewellyn (1987: 4) goes further by suggesting that the term deregulation is at best ambiguous; 'a misnomer and not an accurate description of what is happening in this country or elsewhere.' He notes that the regulation of financial institutions can take a number of forms, and what we have witnessed in Britain is re-regulation, or a change in the regulatory mix, not deregulation. In many ways the regulatory environment in which financial institutions operate has become more formalised and detailed. Traditionally, regulation in Britain has been self-imposed by the use of mechanisms such as cartels, restrictive practices and self-regulatory associations. In recent years the nature of the regulation has become more formalised, explicit and interventionist through the use of legislation and self-regulatory and supervisory bodies. The most important illustration of this shift in emphasis is the Financial Services Act 1986, and its precursor the Gower Report (see Lomax 1987 for a more detailed account).

The purpose of the Gower Report, commissioned by the government and published in 1984, was to consider the issue of investor protection. Two main issues were addressed. The first was the treatment given to investors by life assurance and unit trusts salespeople, in particular whether they were selling appropriate financial products to meet the consumer's needs rather than selling those for which they gained the most commission. The second issue addressed the growing problem of small investment companies going bankrupt, or where the proprietor absconded taking investors' savings. The report concluded that consumers did need some additional protection. Market forces alone could not assure investor protection. However, the report maintained that self-regulation was the most appropriate form of regulation, and that self-regulatory organisations should be established and financed by the financial services industry, not the tax payer.

The Gower Report proved to be the forerunner of the 1986 Financial Services Act, which provided a new and sophisticated system for the regulation of investment business in Britain. At the time the Financial Services Bill was published, the Trade and Industry Secretary, Leon Brittan, stated 'The Government's objective is to create a system of regulation which is both flexible and inspires confidence in investors that the financial services sector is a clean place to do business' (cited in Lever 1992: 259). The main thrust of the Act was that of self or practitioner-based regulation in a statutory context. The Act was based upon what was considered the best practice from Britain, combined with the regulatory experience of the US since 1934 (Blair 1991). It aimed to ensure that investment managers and advisers were 'fit and proper' to conduct business, and that what had long been regarded as 'good practice' was put on a statutory footing. The Act replaced a Department of Trade and Industry licensing system with one that required a much tighter entry procedure. To gain authorisation companies had to be accepted as a member of one of four regulatory bodies established under the terms of the Act. Those self-regulatory organisations (SROs) consist of the Financial Intermediaries Managers and Brokers Regulatory Association

(FIMBRA), Investment Managers Regulatory Organisation (IMRO), Life Assurance and Unit Trust Regulatory Organisation (LAUTRO) and the Securities and Futures Association (SFA). The Securities and Investment Board was set up to authorise investment business and regulate the SROs. Each SRO has its own complaints procedure, although the schemes differ in the way they are organised (see McGee 1992).

Despite the extensive reforms brought about by the Financial Services Act, it has not been universally well received. Blair (1991) has commented on three main weaknesses. First, many of the new procedures associated with the terms of the Act are expensive, especially for small companies (see also Office of Fair Trading 1987). Second, because of the large number of bodies involved in the self-regulatory arrangements, it has produced a certain amount of overlapping of membership and functions. Finally, the Act has been perceived as being too long, too detailed and too prescriptive, and not being able to distinguish adequately between 'the protection properly required for the private consumer and that less intrusive amount required for institutional business' (Blair 1991: 2). More recently, there have been calls from consumer groups to address issues which were not contained in the Act. They have argued that the commission paid to independent advisors should be disclosed to consumers. This would enable consumers to determine whether there was any bias in the salesperson's presentation. This issue was recently investigated by the Office of Fair Trading (1992a) in its report *Independent Financial Advisors and the Impact of Commission Disclosure*. Consumer groups have also pressed for the banning of unsolicited calls to sell life assurance and unit trusts. However, the effectiveness of the Act can be assessed by the way it has protected investors against financial loss since its introduction. According to that criterion the Act is left wanting. A number of significant failures have occurred on a scale hitherto unknown in financial service history in Britain. The Barlow Clowes affair, the Maxwell pensions scandal, the Bank of Credit and Commerce International fraud and the collapse of the Polly Peck empire all suggest that there is no room for complacency where consumer protection is concerned.

An alternative method of financial service regulation introduced in the 1990s was through the mechanism of voluntary codes of practice. In January 1987, the Chancellor of the Exchequer and the Governor of the Bank of England appointed what became known as the Jacks Committee to undertake a review of law and practice in the banking industry. The Committee's central recommendation was that providers of banking services (which included building societies) should prepare and adopt a code of banking practice. The first draft, presented in December 1990, was not well received by consumer groups and the Banking Ombudsman. It was considered 'over-protective of the banks' position' and did not go far enough (Jacks 1992: 3). A year later the Code was published in its final form and incorporated five main themes:

1 that banks and building societies should act 'fairly and reasonably' in their dealings with customers;
2 a ban of the charges on charges scenario whereby because a customer goes overdrawn through paying charges on one period, they incur charges on the next;
3 the maximum liability for money taken from any type of plastic card without the cardholder's agreement was restricted to £50, and nil if a new card was lost or stolen before it reaches the owner;
4 personal financial details would not be passed on to separate non-banking companies within a banking group, such as an insurance and unit trust subsidiary;
5 banks which sign up for the Code should belong to the Banking Ombudsman scheme (the membership of the Building Society Ombudsman scheme being required by law); and all institutions must set up their own internal complaints procedure.

The final Code, which included many of the themes neglected in the original draft, came into effect in March 1992. By 30 April 1992, 237 banks and 90 building societies had adopted the Code.

In the 1980s consumer organisations pressed for the establishment of an efficient complaints and compensation scheme in the financial service industry. To a large extent this request has been fulfilled by the advent of Financial Service Ombudsmen. This aspect of consumer redress is discussed further in the next section.

## FINANCIAL SERVICE OMBUDSMEN SCHEMES

During the decade 1981–91, all four of the Financial Service Ombudsmen schemes currently in operation were introduced. The schemes include all the important financial service industries: insurance and unit trusts; banking; building societies; and pensions. The schemes reflect a growing awareness and emphasis on consumer rights and redress in the financial services sector in Britain. Shurman (1991: 65–6) has indicated that prior to the introduction of these schemes, the individual consumer was in a much weaker position in terms of complaining about financial service institutions. Civil courts were not a suitable forum for the resolution of complaints such as those which are brought before Financial Service Ombudsmen. Shirman notes that 'courts are too slow, too legalistic and too intimidating' and for many consumers they are too expensive. However, he has stressed that the role of the Ombudsman is not that of 'consumer champion', but of an 'impartial and independent conciliator and adjudicator' (ibid.).

The growing number of complaints brought before the Ombudsmen gives an indication of how satisfied some consumers are with the service they receive from financial service providers. It should be stressed, however, that consumers are encouraged by all the Ombudsmen schemes to consult with their financial service provider, and to go through all their internal complaints procedures, before the Ombudsman can take any further action. The complaints dealt with by the Ombudsmen should be viewed as the 'tip of the iceberg' in relation to the overall number of complaints made by consumers. An extensive analysis of the legal aspects of all the Financial Service Ombudsmen schemes has been documented elsewhere (McGee 1992). The intention in the following review is to provide some details of the membership of the schemes and their terms of reference, and to examine the extent to which they are being used by consumers to complain.

## Insurance Ombudsman and Unit Trust Ombudsman

The Insurance Ombudsman Bureau was established in March 1981, and was the first Financial Service Ombudsman scheme in Britain. It was developed and funded by a number of insurance companies which, according to Morgan and Knights (1992), set up the scheme as part of a package of measures to avoid government regulation. Since 1991 the Office of the Insurance Ombudsman has been combined with the office of the Unit Trust Ombudsman. According to McGee (1992), the merger was pre-empted by the small number of complaints received by the Unit Trust Ombudsman. However, contrary to this, Mitchell (1991b) has argued that a major reason for the amalgamation was the lack of support from the industry. The Insurance Ombudsman scheme is voluntary. Insurance companies are not compelled to join, although most do. In November 1992, there were 344 members, which covered around 90 per cent of personal insurance business as measured by premium income. The scheme provides an independent and impartial method of resolving disputes between insurers and individual policy holders, and between individuals and unit trust management companies. The scheme excludes commercial policies, whether they be held by companies, partnerships or

*Table 6.1* Complaints analysis:* Insurance Ombudsman, 1992

|  | Total | % of total |
|---|---|---|
| Life assurances | 1,079 | 24.1 |
| Motor | 842 | 18.8 |
| Household: buildings | 646 | 14.5 |
| Household: contents | 576 | 12.9 |
| Personal accident/sickness/ loan protection | 354 | 7.9 |
| Total | 3,497 | 78.2 |

*Source:* Insurance Ombudsman (1992).
*Note:* * Figures relate to top five categories only.

sole traders. The complaints procedure operates on a free-of-charge basis, and the insurance industry has collectively accepted that any ruling made by the Ombudsman should be abided by.

In 1992 the Insurance Ombudsman received 4,476 complaints, as opposed to 2,839 in 1991. In most cases (2,897 out of 4,476) the insurer's decision was upheld. Payments to claimants as a result of the Ombudsman's awards totalled approximately £4.5 million. The largest individual decision involved a payment of £120,000. The five categories which generated the most complaints in 1992 were life assurance, household buildings, household contents, personal accident and sickness loan protection (see Table 6.1).

## The Banking Ombudsman scheme

The Banking Ombudsman scheme was set up in 1986. Any consumer who has received a banking service is eligible to submit a complaint to the Banking Ombudsman. This facility exists whether or not the complainant is a customer of the particular bank in question. In contrast with the Insurance Ombudsman Bureau, the Banking Ombudsman also includes sole traders, partnerships and clubs. The Ombudsman's terms of reference enable all types of business transacted through bank branches of member banks to be assessed. The Ombudsman has the power to make binding awards up to a value of £100,000. At the end of September 1992, thirty-six banks were members of the scheme, including all the major high street banks and their subsidiaries. Around 99 per cent of all bank account holders are covered by the scheme.

The number of complaints has increased substantially over the time since the scheme was introduced. In 1987, 1,682 new complaints were

*Table 6.2* Complaints analysis:* Banking Ombudsman, 1992

|  | Total | % of total |
|---|---|---|
| Charges and interest | 1,939 | 19.2 |
| Lending | 1,464 | 14.5 |
| ATMs | 879 | 8.7 |
| Account errors | 680 | 6.7 |
| Credit/debit cards | 641 | 6.4 |
| Total | 5,603 | 55.5 |

*Source:* Banking Ombudsman Scheme (1991–2).
*Note:* * Figures relate to top five categories only.

received by 1992 this figure had risen to 9,425. There has also been a sharp increase in 'mature' (more serious) complaints in the period 1987–92. Mature in this sense indicates the need for the Ombudsman to take the complaint further and instigate a full investigation. This is in contrast to 'immature' complaints which have not reached the 'deadlock' stage, and are often resolved by member banks without further intervention by the Ombudsman. By far the most frequent complaints in 1992 related to interest and charges, followed by lending, automatic teller machines and account errors (see Table 6.2).

**The Building Society Ombudsman scheme**

The Building Society Ombudsman scheme was set up according to the terms of the Building Societies Act 1986, which indicated that all building societies should be members of an approved Ombudsman scheme. The range of activities investigated by the Building Society Ombudsman are set out in Part II of schedule 12 of the 1986 Act. They are described under the following headings:

  share accounts
  deposit accounts
  borrowing members
  class 1 or class 2 advances
  borrowers: loans by appropriate mortgage companies
  borrowers: mobile home loans
  borrowers: other loans
  banking services
  trusteeship
  executorship

*Table 6.3* Complaints analysis:* Building Society Ombudsman, 1992–3

|  | Total |
|---|---|
| Insurance | 1,062 |
| Investment interest rates | 809 |
| Current account facilities | 721 |
| Problems about mortgage repayments | 552 |
| Mortgage arrears | 435 |
| Total | 3,579 |

*Source:* Building Societies Ombudsman Scheme (1992–3).
*Note:* * Figures relate to top five categories only.

The Building Society Ombudsman scheme has the power to pay compensation up to a value of £100,000. However, because of the statutory nature of the scheme, it is not appropriate to make Ombudsman decisions binding on members. The terms of reference allow building societies to escape from the obligation to comply with the Ombudsman's decision. However, they must circulate a note of refusal, and a statement indicating the reasons why, to other members.

The number of complaints brought to the attention of the Ombudsman has increased considerably. In its first year, a total of 980 complaints and other communications were received. By 1992–93, 9,402 initial complaints and enquiries were received. The most frequently cited complaints were related to insurance, investment rates and current account facilities (see Table 6.3).

## Pensions Ombudsman

The Pensions Ombudsman scheme came into effect on 2 April 1991, following the Social Security Act 1990. The scheme is statutory rather than voluntary. The Ombudsman's terms of reference facilitate the investigation of complaints caused by 'maladministration by the trustees or managers of occupational or personal pension schemes, and disputes of fact or law with the trustees or managers' (McGee 1992: 48). National insurance retirement pensions and most other public service pension schemes are not covered. The scheme does cover occupational pensions (those operated by employers) and private pensions.

As with the other Ombudsmen schemes, consumers must first attempt to settle the dispute with the company concerned. If this fails, the next step is for the complainant to take the matter to the Occupational Pensions Advisory Service (OPAS). This is a voluntary organisation which has

*Table 6.4* Enquiries analysis: Occupational Pensions Advisory Service, 1991–2

|  | % of total |
| --- | --- |
| Benefits on leaving service, including transfers | 24 |
| Clarification of entitlements and membership conditions | 20 |
| Winding up, mergers and use of surplus funds | 14 |
| Delays in payment and non-response of scheme authorities | 9 |
| Ill health and early retirement | 7 |
| Additional voluntary contributions | 5 |
| Commutation of pensions | 1 |
| Miscellaneous | 20 |
| Total | 100 |

*Source:* Occupational Pensions Advisory Service (1991–2).

local advisors throughout the country who have proven expertise in pensions. Only when this procedure has been undertaken can the Pensions Ombudsman consider the complaint. The Ombudsman's decision is final and is binding on both parties. In 1991–92 forty-seven cases were referred to the Pensions Ombudsman by OPAS. However, OPAS dealt with 20,034 enquires, up from 7,240 in 1991, an increase of 177 per cent. Table 6.4 indicates the nature of occupational and personal enquiries brought to the attention of OPAS.

## FINANCIAL OMBUDSMAN SCHEMES: AN EVALUATION

Financial Service Ombudsman schemes have become a useful avenue of consumer redress. They have afforded consumers the opportunity to pursue claims against financial institutions free-of-charge, without the expense of seeking legal action through the courts. More consumers have used Financial Service Ombudsmen, as the rapidly expanding number of consumer complaints and enquiries testifies. However, whether the Ombudsmen schemes have been as effective as they might have been is debatable. Mitchell (1991b) has suggested that consumer awareness of the Financial Service Ombudsmen schemes is not particularly high. The Office of Fair Trading's 1990 *Annual Consumer Complaints Survey* indicated that only 27 per cent of a national random sample of consumers knew of the existence of the Insurance Ombudsman, 24 per cent the Banking Ombudsman and 22 per cent had heard of the Building Society Ombudsman (Office of Fair Trading 1991). Mitchell has also commented on the lack of active marketing of the Financial Service Ombudsmen schemes by members. Often advertising has been carried out in a low key way. A case in point was the first Building Society Ombudsman's *Annual Report*, which documented that forty building societies had failed to respond to the Ombudsman's request for them to publicly display Ombudsman literature in their branches. Similarly, no society accepted the Ombudsman's view that information about the Ombudsman scheme should be included on the back of customer statements. Further research on the publicity given to the Ombudsman schemes by banks and building societies has been undertaken by Graham *et al.* (1993). They found that banks publicised the Ombudsman scheme and their own internal complaints procedure far more than building societies. Even the large building societies did not publicise the scheme to the same extent as the banks.

Despite the extensive use of the Financial Service Ombudsmen by consumers, there has been little assessment of the profile of consumers that have used the schemes, or an evaluation of the schemes' effectiveness in dealing with complaints. One recent assessment of the Office of the Building Society Ombudsman and the Insurance Ombudsman Bureau was conducted by the National Consumer Council (NCC) (1993b). The NCC survey was based on 938 postal questionnaires returned by consumers whose cases had been assessed by the respective schemes. In relation to the Office of the Building Society Ombudsman, the majority of users were people from professional and managerial backgrounds. Men were three times more likely to use the scheme than women, and over a third of complainants were over 55 years of age. The main complaint about the scheme was that it was too slow. The same criticism was also made of the Insurance scheme, and some respondents were concerned about its independence and fairness. An extensive list of recommendations were set out by the NCC. They dealt with issues about improving information and public accountability, monitoring and improving fairness, and speeding up the decision-making process, among others.

While the Ombudsman schemes have become an important consumer redress facility, there appears to be substantial room for improvement. However, the evaluation of the Financial Service Ombudsmen schemes highlights another important theme of the 1980s and 1990s, that of the increasing attention being given to the welfare of financial service consumers by consumer groups. This issue is discussed further in the final section of the chapter.

## CONSUMERS' GROUPS AND FINANCIAL SERVICES

Consumers' groups have played an important part in promoting the interests of financial service consumers. The Consumers' Association and the National Consumer Council have been particularly active in promoting the consumer's point of view on financial service issues. The political pressure wielded by consumer groups has been perceived by some financial service companies to have a considerable impact on their public image. This function was recognised in the early 1980s.

> Customers have more choices now and more of them are becoming sophisticated, particularly in cash flow management. They are less locked into particular institutions and they are getting increasing support from consumerist opinion and from legislation which supports the consumerist viewpoint.
>
> (Read 1982: 4)

Throughout the 1980s and 1990s financial service firms were faced with a barrage of criticism from consumers and consumer groups. The banks were faced with actively marketing their credibility as producers to consumers, a situation previously unheard of. Similar trends have also been observed in the UK life insurance industry (Morgan and Knights 1992).

The Consumers' Association and its *Which?* magazine were established in Britain in 1957, around twenty years later than its sister organisation in the US. It soon became apparent that the monthly *Which?* magazine could not carry all the topics about which consumers wanted information. Other magazines were added as quarterly supplements: *Motoring Which?* (1962); *Money Which?* (1968); *Handyman Which?* (1971) and *Holiday Which?* (1974) (Gorse 1978). The Consumers' Associations *Which?* and *Money Which?* provide detailed advice on an extensive range of financial service products. The *Which?* magazine regularly features articles on savings, bank accounts and holiday and car insurance. The Association's subscription base is made up largely of middle-class individuals, although magazines are available through public libraries. However, more importantly, the Consumers' Association has brought issues of consumer protection to the forefront of public debate via the media, sponsoring Private Member's Bills, and making their research findings available to the national press.

One of the most lengthy campaigns promoted by the Consumers' Association was the four year action to have a Code of Banking Practice implemented in Britain. The first draft of the voluntary Code was considered 'wholly inadequate'. While the Consumers' Association welcomed the final Code, they indicated a number of deficiencies and the need for further improvement. One area which was not covered was the lack of advanced warning that charges and interest were to be deducted from a consumer's account. Nor does the Code give consumers the right to choose their own Personal Identification Number (PIN), or to collect new cards from their own bank or building society. Also absent was a formal commitment to improving security standards of cash dispensers and PINs. The Consumers' Association were also concerned that banks and building societies had two years to implement the scheme fully. They considered the proposed time scale was 'far too long – it's already 3 years since the first proposed Code was published' (Consumers' Association 1992: 172). The Consumers' Association has also provided an important way by which new processes and products can be evaluated. For example, a recent feature in *Which?*, 'Banking from Home' (Consumers' Association 1993), indicated that stronger security systems needed to be implemented into home banking systems. If something goes wrong with the system, consumers have virtually no right to compensation. The article recommended that in view of the larger numbers of consumers that were using home banking services, the Code of Banking Practice needed to be amended.

A similar lobbying function has been performed by the National Consumer Council (NCC). Several particularly influential reports have been published such as *Banking Services and the Consumer* (1983) and *Credit, Debit and the Consumer Interest* (1990). The NCC has also critically evaluated a number of policy documents such as the Banking Code of Practice (NCC 1991c). It has responded to the research findings of both the Monopolies and Mergers Commission on the issue of credit card services (1987), and the Office of Fair Trading relating to extortionate credit (1991b). More recently, the NCC has become involved in consumer issues which have emerged as a result of the Single European Market. One of these was the *Response to the Draft Directive on the Liability for Services* (1991a), and a directory of consumer advice services in the European Community (1993a).

The activities of consumer groups have led to a more detailed appraisal of consumer issues within the financial services sector. This activity has led to new sets of concerns about the appropriate role and behaviour of financial institutions in modern, Western societies. There have already been a number of debates around the issue of business ethics and social responsibility in the financial services sector (Etkins 1992; Burke *et al*. 1993). Particular emphasis has been given to the ethical issues associated with the provision and cost of consumer credit (Browne 1991; Mahoney 1991). However, these discussions are not confined to Britain; many other European societies are debating the same issues (Reifner and Ford 1992a). Mitchell (1992a) has argued that the changing environment will renew emphasis on financial institutions to become more socially responsible. Banks and other financial institutions have already been pressured to refrain from 'unfair or oppressive' business practices. He predicts that there will be more emphasis on providing banking services to the whole community, including low and moderate income families, because of the disadvantages associated with not having access to core financial services in modern, capitalist societies. He considers that a higher priority should be given to consumers with literacy and numeracy difficulties which may make it problematic for them to understand complex financial service systems. There should also be positive programmes aimed at fostering equality of opportunity both in relation to gender and to race. Finally, more account needs to be taken of physically disabled and sensory impaired consumers, for whom the layout of branches and administrative procedures are demanding and challenging.

## CONCLUSION

Since the 1980s consumer issues and consumer protection have been given a much higher profile within the financial services sector in Britain. This trend is also observable in a number of other OECD countries. Contrary to the philosophy behind much of the Conservative government's policies in the 1980s and 1990s, unfettered market forces have not been considered a sufficient or appropriate way to protect financial service consumers. Underlying the Financial Services Act 1986 was the issue of consumer protection. The setting up of Financial Service Ombudsmen schemes gave consumers a means of redressing the balance between individual consumers and large, economically powerful institutions. Finally, consumer movements were extremely active and effective in moving forward debates about consumer issues and protection.

Given these recent events, the issue which needs addressing is whether the power relations between financial institutions and consumers has significantly altered in recent years. This debate is the focus of attention in the next chapter.

# SUMMARY

The financial service environment in Britain has become much more consumer friendly since the 1980s. There are a number of reasons for this:

1 legislative changes which have increased the level of consumer protection;
2 The introduction of financial ombudsmen schemes;
3 the activities of consumer groups which have supported the consumer's point of view.

# Chapter 7

# Consumer: king or peasant?

Financial service organisations gave personal sector consumers a much higher profile in the 1980s and 1990s. The increasingly competitive marketplace resulting from the decline in traditional boundaries between financial service providers, combined with manufacturers and retailers moving into the financial service market, were all important factors in the increased consumer orientation. Banks, building societies and insurance companies transformed themselves into financial supermarkets and promoted an extensive range of products. The rate of product innovation in the industry has been rapid, as organisations have searched for something new and novel to entice consumers. Traditional market research techniques have been used to segment the mass market and this has enabled products to be tailored to meet individual consumer's needs. Financial service institutions, in common with many other retailers, have also begun to promote products that are 'green' or ethically sound in an attempt to attract additional consumers. However, whether such initiatives have equated with a fundamental change in the balance of power within the producer–consumer relationship, whereby consumers have become more powerful, is doubtful. Rather, such moves appear indicative of the relative profitability of different types of financial service business. Following the Third World debt crisis in the 1970s and early 1980s, the increasingly competitive international banking markets and several periods of recession which adversely affected the profitability of corporate banking, personal sector consumers were one of the few remaining profitable areas.

The intervention of important 'actors' supporting the consumer interest has been a notable trend in Britain since the 1980s. Consumer groups have been very vocal, and pressed hard for reforms and more accountability on the part of financial institutions. The 1980s was also the decade when Financial Service Ombudsmen schemes were established to provide an additional avenue of consumer redress. Financial service legislation also reflected a preoccupation with protecting the consumer interest. Had financial service organisations genuinely become more consumer-led, many of the activities designed to promote the consumer interest would not have been necessary.

The view that the power relations between producers and consumers has shifted in favour of consumers will be critically evaluated in this chapter. The first section considers evidence from recent trends in Britain, while the rest of the chapter concentrates on the impact of the Single European Market (SEM).

## POWER RELATIONS WITHIN THE CONSUMER–PRODUCER RELATIONSHIP IN BRITAIN

Clearly, there have been a number of ways in which financial institutions have become more consumer-orientated in the 1980s and 1990s. However, it is not clear that there has been a fundamental shift in the power relations between financial service producers and consumers. A number of indicators suggest that financial services producers are still incredibly powerful institutions, and that recent changes have done little to affect the power dynamics within the consumer–producer relationship in Britain. Ultimately, there are fewer producers from which consumers can buy financial services in Britain than there has ever been. At the end of the last century, there were literally hundreds of banks in Britain (Collins 1991), and over 2,000 building societies existed (Drake 1989). There has been a severe contraction in the number of banks, building societies and insurance companies as a result of mergers and acquisitions and as a response to increasingly competitive conditions. The largest annual rate of decline in the number of building societies this century occurred between 1980–6, a reduction of 9.7 per cent (Drake 1989). Similarly, the numbers of investment brokers registered to give independent advice has plummeted as a result of the Financial Services Act 1986. The number of clearing banks from which consumers can choose is also small. This situation appears at odds with changes in the regulatory environment which has aimed at giving consumers a wider choice of producers from which to purchase financial services. The situation in the financial service sector in Britain appears to support Keat's (1991) view that consumers had more power in the era of industrial capitalism when small organisations competed with each other for business. In response to the concentration of financial institutions into a smaller number of large companies, there is further concern about the lack of price and product competition. This is still apparent in Britain, where most financial service firms offer similar services, at similar prices.

Following on from the trend of fewer financial service suppliers, there has also been a decline in the number of branch offices from which consumers can purchase financial services. As a result of increased competition, organisations have attempted to reduce their cost:income ratios by rationalising their costly branch structures. The number of bank branches in Britain has decreased substantially in recent years. In 1980 there were 14,767 bank branches; by 1992 that figure had decreased to 12,500 (figures exclude Girobank). The numbers of building society branches have also declined. In 1980 there were 5,684 building society offices, which increased to nearly 7,000 in the mid-1980s. By 1991 the number of building society offices had declined to 5,921 (Committee of London and Scottish Bankers 1988; British Bankers' Association 1993). However, this decline in branch offices is not just apparent in Britain, but other parts of Europe as well (FIET 1984). It is arguably the case that fewer branches could be regarded as inconvenience for consumers. It is also overwhelmingly the case that many branches are concentrated on high street sites. Few financial institutions have ventured to out-of-town shopping centres and industrial estates where few financial service facilities exist. In the 1990s Britain's financial service consumers are not only faced with fewer branches, but those that remain are highly concentrated in often inconvenient locations such as city and town centres, and high street sites (Burton 1990). There is obviously a tension here between financial service providers wishing to present themselves as being more consumer-orientated, which would ideally mean more branches and staff, and the additional costs that would generate. Furthermore, this is an issue which consumers and consumer organisations can do little to change.

While the increased use of information technology has provided financial service consumers with considerable benefits, such as ATMs, EFTPOS, home and telephone banking, it has also given financial service producers an enormously powerful method of surveillance. It is now common for consumers, when opening an account, to be subject to credit referencing which would highlight County Court judgments. This procedure is often undertaken as a matter of routine, even if the consumer wants to open an account which involves no lending facility, such as a savings account. In most instances, financial service producers also wish to receive a satisfactory report or reference from a former provider with whom the consumer has had a previous 'relationship' before granting facilities. This suggests that banks and other financial institutions both individually and collectively operate a network of control which gives them considerable power over consumers.

The use of information technology in the credit scoring process has also been a major way in which producers have used surveillance techniques to control the activities of consumers. Traditionally, lenders sought to minimise lending risks by examining an individual's character, capacity and collateral, and by obtaining references. However, the high volume of lending assessments required to meet the needs of contemporary consumers has meant that information technology has been used to assess the degree of risk involved. In many ways credit scoring has removed, rather than encouraged, flexibility between producers. There have been few studies which have systematically assessed the variability of credit scoring outcomes between different institutions, and it is an avenue of enquiry which needs further consideration. However, because of the relatively uniform design of credit scoring systems, it is highly likely that if a consumer fails a credit scoring exercise at one financial institution, it is conceivable that they will also fail at another. Automated credit scoring has, in many instances, removed the space for managerial discussion and added to the strength of the producer against the consumer. An Office of Fair Trading (1992b) report on the issue of credit scoring also identified a trend towards generic bureau scoring systems which could produce a greater uniformity to lenders' decisions than exists at present. It has been the usual practice in Britain for financial institutions to consult a credit reference agency for information which can then be built into their own credit scoring systems. Generic bureau scoring systems provide financial institutions with an actual decision rather than information. If this practice was extended, producers would have even more control over consumers than they have at present. This is particularly disturbing for certain sections of the population who may be discriminated against because of their social and economic characteristics. From this viewpoint, the 'new' ideology of the person-alised service delivery must be called into question.

A key theme of the 1980s and 1990s was the importance of quality in the service delivery. To this end, financial institutions segmented their workforce into specialists such as counsellor, mortgage advisor and so on. The aim of such moves was to give the consumer a more professional, quality service delivery. However, at the other end of the spectrum there has been an increase in the use of part-time staff. This trend has also been noted within financial institutions in other European countries (FIET 1987). Several studies of the banks (Robinson 1985; MacInnes 1988; Burton 1992) and building societies (Crompton and Sanderson 1990) have indicated that part-time employees have less knowledge and skills than their full-time colleagues. Yet part-timers are frequently employed in roles which have a high degree of consumer contact at peak times of the day, week or year. It appears that rather than employing and training staff in a wider range of skills and abilities to meet the needs of demanding consumers, there is a large group of employees within the clerical strata for which the opposite is true. This brings the claims made by financial institutions that they provide a high quality service for consumers into doubt. The transition towards numerical flexibility through the use of part-timers is one of a range of cost-cutting measures which has reduced the overall skill density within financial institutions. This is a trend which cannot be in the consumer's best interest.

Whether or not the power relations between financial service producers and consumers in Britain has significantly altered in the consumer's favour is a contentious issue. It has been argued that despite financial service institutions becoming more consumer orientated to attract new business, the power within the producer-consumer relationship has remained firmly with the producers in a number of fundamental ways. The advent of the Single European Market has been deemed as being of monumental importance in giving consumers much more choice and value for money. Whether or not the SEM will provide consumers with more power in their dealings with financial service producers is discussed in the next section.

## THE SINGLE EUROPEAN MARKET AND THE CONSUMER: FRIEND OR FOE?

The benefits of the SEM for consumers is an issue which has received considerable attention in recent years. Most of the discussion on this issue has focused upon research undertaken by Price Waterhouse, 'The Cost of a Non-Europe in Financial Services', more widely known as the Cecchini Report. The Cecchini Report surveyed the prices of a range of standard banking, insurance and brokerage services across Europe. Some of the products surveyed related to services purchased by companies, others to private individuals. The personal sector financial service products surveyed in the research are listed in Table 7.1. For each of the countries in the study, the product prices were estimated on the basis of surveying a sample of market participants, and then converting the price to ECU which enabled inter-country comparisons to be made. The average of the four lowest prices was taken to be the lowest competitive standard for each of the eight countries. The extent to which the price of different

*Table 7.1* Consumer financial services surveyed in the Cecchini Report

| Name of standard service | Description of standard service |
| --- | --- |
| Consumer credit | Annual cost of a 500 ECU loan |
| Credit cards | Annual cost of a 500 ECU debit |
| Mortgages | Annual cost of a 25,000 ECU home loan |
| Travellers cheques | Cost of purchasing 500 ECU |
| Life insurance | Average annual cost of term (life) insurance |
| Home Insurance | Fire and theft cover for a house valued at 70,000 ECU, with 28,000 ECU contents |
| Motor insurance | Comprehensive insurance for a 1.6 litre car, driver ten years' experience, no claims bonus |

*Source:* Adapted from Emerson (1988).

*Table 7.2* Estimated falls in financial product prices following the implementation of the Single European Market

| | B | D | E | F | I | L | NL | UK |
| --- | --- | --- | --- | --- | --- | --- | --- | --- |
| | | | | % | | | | |
| Consumer credit | −41 | 136 | 39 | 105 | Na* | −26 | 31 | 121 |
| Credit cards | 79 | 60 | 26 | −30 | 89 | −12 | 43 | 16 |
| Mortgages | 31 | 57 | 118 | 78 | −4 | Na* | −6 | −20 |
| Travellers cheques | 35 | −7 | 30 | 39 | 22 | −7 | 33 | −7 |
| Life insurance | 78 | 5 | 37 | 33 | 83 | 66 | −9 | −30 |
| Home insurance | −16 | 3 | −4 | 39 | 81 | 57 | 17 | 90 |
| Motor insurance | 30 | 15 | 100 | 9 | 148 | 77 | −7 | −17 |

*Source:* Adapted from Emerson (1988).
*Note:* * Na = exact figures not available, estimates used.

financial service products varied from this standard are given in Table 7.2. The cost of consumer credit in the UK and Germany was more expensive than other countries in the sample. It is likely that the cost of credit will be reduced in Britain with the advent of the SEM. On the other hand, the price of life insurance in the UK was much cheaper than most other countries, whereas home insurance was very expensive.

Despite the benefits of the SEM for consumers claimed in the Cecchini Report, there has been some scepticism as to whether the projected advantages will in fact materialise and, if they do occur, what the time scale will be. A number of difficulties with the report have been highlighted. The first has related to the methodology employed in the study. The Cecchini research methodology involved identifying a range of standardised financial service products in each of the Member States.

Then each country's prices were compared with the average of the four lowest. The difference was then used to indicate whether the price paid for a particular product would be likely to decrease or increase within each Member State. However, this formula has been criticised because the bench mark price did not relate to the actual price that consumers in any of the Members States were paying. This has led some commentators to suggest that the Cecchini results may be subject to large margins of error. Difficulties also arise with choosing a selection of financial service products across the EC because, in practice, financial service products cannot always be standardised and this can make precise comparisons impossible. For example, the cost of insurance premiums may reflect different degrees of risk and mortality within different Member States and this is a cultural as much as an economic phenomenon. The cross-sectional research design also lacked any longitudinal component. Consequently, the research gave no indication of price fluctuations over time, which would have been a useful indicator in projecting future price changes.

Another point of dispute has been the Cecchini Report's assumption that price differentials in Member States resulted from a lack of market competition. Llewellyn (1992) has argued that this is not necessarily the case, and that a number of factors maybe relevant. These may include differences in efficiency, rent costs, internal bundling and cross-subsidisation (made possible by the development of multi-product financial service firms operating in markets with different groups of consumers), the non-exploitation of economies of scale and variation in financial regulation. Similarly, Emerson (1988) has suggested that it is difficult to separate out EC actions to liberalise financial markets from other domestic and international influences which may be pushing in the same direction. Furthermore, they note that even if price differentials were to converge, it would be incorrect to simply pinpoint the outcome to increased levels of competition. Given that price differences cannot be specifically related to low levels of competition, it is not clear that regulatory change associated with the SEM will automatically produce a uniform lower price for financial service products that consumers were promised.

Another of the major advantages predicted by the Cecchini Report was the economies of scale from which financial service organisations would benefit as a result of expansion and diversification. The predicted effect for consumers was increased choice and price reductions. However, Gardener (1992) has questioned whether economies of scale actually exist in the financial services sector in the way described by the Cecchini

Report. He notes that the existence and empirical extent of economies of scale in the banking industry is a debatable issue. Research has indicated that there is no such thing as an optimum size for a bank, and that economies of scale occur in some areas of business, but not others. Similarly, Dixon (1991) has argued that many European banks are already large, and conduct business abroad. He has suggested that if economies of scale were possible, many financial institutions should have already benefited from these advantages before the SEM came into effect. The underlying assumption that large institutions will provide more benefits for consumers is also questionable. Mitchell (1991a: 146), for example, considers 'The worst outcome for consumers would be a series of European super-bank alliances actively protecting high margins in separate national markets.'

Gardener (1992) has also questioned the time scale for the predicted price convergence which the SEM is supposed to generate. He considers it irrational for financial service firms to use a strategy whereby they enter other European markets at a lower price to undercut domestic firms in a bid to attract business for any length of time. He also believes that only large institutions would be able to carry losses until a reputation was established among consumers in the host state. Another way prices might be reduced is if institutions in low price countries expanded abroad to make for uniform lower prices throughout the Community. However, he has suggested that the recent Basle capital adequacy rules are likely to constrain the expansion of European banks, and thus possibly hinder extensive price competition and convergence. In any event, for some financial service products, Britain is already cheaper than many other countries in the EC. The cost of mortgages is a case in point. However, even if mortgage finance could be purchased more cheaply from a European supplier, many consumers may resist the temptation. The purchase of mortgage finance is a long-term relationship, and consumers may well feel it prudent to purchase from a local supplier whom they trust (Holmes 1992). It is not clear that the reduction in prices consumers were promised as a consequence of the SEM will become a reality, or what length of time would be involved if it were to materialise. It would also seem that any price reductions from which consumers could benefit would be in highly selective areas of business, rather than uniform price cuts across the board.

There has also been some doubt as to whether the SEM will have a stimulating effect on the choice of financial service products that are available to consumers. A report by Euromonitor (1992) has suggested that there were few significant differences between the types of products offered by financial institutions in other European Member States. The report concluded that the quality of service and administrative efficiency were much more likely to be a basis of differentiation than the type of financial service product provided. This emphasis on the quality of the service delivery may be an additional reason why the SEM might be something of a misnomer for consumers. The high degree of personal contact which often accompanies the purchase of financial services products could be a decisive factor in consumers remaining loyal to 'local' companies. A priority for many financial firms will be safe-guarding their share in their own national market while simultaneously exploring networking and/or collaborative opportunities with European partners. This sort of defensive strategy may well jeopardise the consumer gains which the single market was designed to generate (Consumers in the European Community Group 1992).

There are also significant differences between EC countries along a number of dimensions and these may cause difficulties in creating a fully integrated SEM for financial services. Llewellyn (1992: 115) has noted that EC national financial systems are far from integrated and significant differences remain in relation to 'regulation, taxation, the competitive environment, exchange control and the role of the state'. There are also significant differences in the ownership and control of financial institutions in different Member states. Many countries have a combination of both public and privately-owned financial institutions, although the balance of each is variable (Broker 1990). At the end of the 1980s around 80–90 per cent of Italian and almost 50 per cent of West German banks were in the public sector (Jones 1989). It is not clear what effect the different combinations of ownership and control have had on the intensity of competition or the ability of financial organisations to become more consumer-led. There are also differences in language and currencies which will act as barriers to cross-border trade. Other non-economic advantages, especially for domestic institutions, are the reputation of financial service institutions and customer loyalty.

The implications of the SEM for financial service consumers is far from clear. However, much of the existing literature treats consumers as though they were an undifferentiated, homogeneous category, which is clearly not so. It may well be the case that the advent of the SEM favours some groups of consumers, but not others. As Vogler states,

> For those groups with higher incomes, more mobility and who are well informed, achieving a broad range of financial offers and assessing them with regard to their positive and negative consequences may be

un-problematic. This, however, is not necessarily the case for those with lower incomes who are poorly informed.

(Vogler 1992: 96)

It is highly likely that middle-class, well-educated consumers who know how to play the financial services system will be the groups of consumers to benefit most from the SEM. Affluent individuals also tend to be the most profitable group of consumers for financial institutions and would be among the first to be singled out by financial service providers in an attempt to attract profitable business in other Member States. However, those consumers would also be the most difficult to group to lure as they would be a profitable group for domestic institutions who will provide incentives to keep them. Rather than the SEM benefiting all consumers, a highly stratified consumer structure could emerge, with high net worth individuals gaining most.

In this section some doubts have been raised about the benefits of the SEM for consumers. Given some of these reservations, the next section will consider to what extent EC consumer policy has been developed to provide protection for financial service consumers.

## EUROPEAN CONSUMER POLICY AND THE FINANCIAL SERVICES SECTOR

The European Community adopted its first consumer programme in 1975. It set out five basic consumer rights:

- The right to protection of economic interests
- The right to information and education
- The right of representation and consultation
- The right to protection of health and safety
- The right to redress

The task of promoting consumer affairs within the EC was originally co-ordinated by the European Commission's Consumer Protection Service, which was part of Directorate-General XI. However, by 1989 the Commission had established the Consumer Policy Service as a distinct and separate division from any other Directorate-General. A three-year action plan, launched in 1990, set out a programme which had three main objectives: to improve people's working and living conditions; to ensure a similar level of consumer protection exists throughout Member States; and to enable consumers to purchase goods and services from anywhere within the EC. Despite the Commission's good intentions, the Consumers in the European Community Group (1991: 15) has indicated that for a number of years the Commission has lacked an effective consumer service, with too few staff attempting to cover too many different policy areas. This lack of commitment by the council has led to 'low staff morale and weakened the ability of the service to influence events'. The Consumers in the European Community Group has also indicated that EC financial support for consumer affairs has been inadequate. In 1991 the Community spent only £9.6 million on consumer protection activities. This figure was to be cut to £3 million in 1992, out of a total Community budget of £43 billion. 'For every penny the EC plans to spend on consumers, it will spend over £3 on encouraging the production of tobacco' (1991: 15).

Another way in which consumer issues have been channelled into EC policy is through the Consumers' Consultative Committee which was established in 1973, and was renamed the Consumers Consultative Council (CCC) in 1990. The CCC meets two to three times a year in Brussels and provides a forum whereby consumer organisations are able to discuss issues of consumer protection with the Community. However, the Consumers in the European Community Group (1991: 15) has been sceptical about the influence the CCC has within the Commission. The infrequent nature of CCC meetings, the lack of 'clout or ability to promote its opinions', given that the Commission has indicated that CCC papers should be regarded as confidential, and its lack of independence because its secretariat is provided by the Commission have all been considered weaknesses. The Consumers in the European Community Group has recommended that

> The CCC should become a European Consumer Council, with an independent Secretariat funded by the Commission. It should be free to promote the CCC's views actively and widely, including by lobbying and press publicity. The Secretariat should be given the resources necessary to carry out this role and make the CCC function properly.
>
> (Consumers in the European Community Group 1992: 18)

In addition to the EC Consumer Policy Service and the CCC, there are also several lobbying organisations which promote the interests of consumers at the pan-European level. One of these is Bureau Européen des Unions de Consommateurs (BEUC) which was set up in 1962 by European consumer organisations. BEUC is the umbrella organisation for all consumer groups within the EC. Similarly, the Confederation of Family Organisations in the EC (COFACE) provides a similar lobbying function. However, both organisations have proved expensive to operate, and have employed a small number of staff who need to cover an extensive range of technical areas. This situation is in stark contrast to the large numbers of specialist Euro-groups supporting the interests of producers. In 1970 around 300 Euro-groups existed, a figure which had risen to 525 by 1992. Of those 525 Euro-groups, it has been estimated that 50 per cent represented industry and commerce, 25 per cent agriculture and food, 20 per cent services and 5 per cent trade unions and other interests (Mazey and Richardson 1992). These statistics lead Mitchell (1993) to conclude that capitalist groups vastly outnumber consumer organisations, and they are well-resourced and organised to protect their interests. Indeed there has been a growing trend for large multinational companies to have their own public relations staff or to hire consultants in Brussels.

At the national level, the Commission has already recognised that the infrastructure of consumer organisations is weaker in some Member States than in others, and this is acting as a barrier to consumer integration. For the most part, consumer organisations are rather better established in the northern countries of the Community than in the south. A directory of consumer advice services in the EC compiled by the National Consumer Council (1993a), also found that there were considerable differences in the 'networks' of advice services within different Member States. Major advice networks were identified in Germany, the Netherlands, Ireland, Italy and the UK. The report recommended that more research effort needed to be deployed in uncovering additional advice services and in identifying 'gaps' in existing provision. Local advice services often provided a 'front-line' function in protecting the consumer interest and, given that consumer complaints could increase and become more complex with the advent of the Single European Market, this activity should be given a higher priority. It was therefore ironic that EC plans to provide financial support for developing consumer representation in southern Europe were cancelled. Mitchell (1991a: 150) has also indicated that a number of other retrograde steps are in the pipeline, including:

- Cutting off financial support to consumer organisations;
- Dissolving the CCC (Consumers' Consultative Council);
- Stopping all new studies of how the Single Market will affect consumers;
- Closing down trans-border consumer information centres and projects for resolving consumer complaints.

The apparent indifferent attitude towards consumer issues at the EC level is reinforced in relation to the financial services sector. In his book *Banker's Racket or Consumer Benefit?*, Mitchell (1991a) has set out a number of shortcomings of the Single Market for consumers. At the core of EC policy in the financial services sector are three freedoms: the free movement of capital; the freedom of establishment; and the freedom to supply services. He notes that the 'consumer's freedom to buy services is not stated explicitly' (1991a: 148). The emphasis throughout negotiations has been to provide a structure which has facilitated the freedom of financial institutions, not the consumer. He argues that the Commission should take steps to construct a fourth freedom, a freedom to enable consumers to purchase financial services without national or residential discrimination. A similar low profile has been given to the issue of consumer protection. Lamb's (1991) assessment of community legislation affecting the banking sector and banking transactions concluded that three principal areas had been highlighted: banking supervision; accountancy; and consumer protection. Of these three, he noted 'banking supervision has emerged as the primary focus of attention in the lead up to "1992" ' (1991: 2).

Financial services as a group of industries have not featured prominently within the context of pan-European consumer groups. Consumer groups which have been successful in attracting attention have been in traditional industries such as coal, steel and agriculture (Mazey and Richardson 1992). Consumer groups have therefore been in a weak position to affect change because of this lack of a track record. Mitchell (1991a) has suggested that the pressure to complete the SEM by the end of 1992 has meant that Commission officials have negotiated with representatives of financial service organisations early to prevent any delays at a later stage. This emphasis on acquiring an acceptable outcome for financial service producers has meant that Commission officials have often neglected to consult consumer groups and have not made working documents available for their comment.

The Consumers in the European Community Group, in its paper *EC Framework for Financial Services* (1992), has also identified a number of shortcomings in consumer policy as it applies to financial services. The group has argued that before purchasing financial service products, it is imperative that consumers understand the full extent of their rights and obligations and that these should be stated in jargon-free language. This is particularly important with financial products such as pensions and mortgages, which are long-term commitments. However, as far as the SEM is concerned, there are 'no harmonised rules on the content of contracts between suppliers of financial services and consumers, although some directives will require pre-contractual disclosure of key information' (1992: 6). Another important issue has related to the availability of consumer redress procedures. The industry-based Financial Service Ombudsmen schemes are an important part of the consumer redress procedure in Britain. Other Member States, although not all, also have industry-based complaints schemes. However, there has been little evidence to date of cross-border co-operation in formulating terms of reference and procedures. As the report states

> It is unclear whether a French firm which provides cross-border services without being established in the UK will be eligible for membership of a voluntary UK scheme. If it is not, and there is no equivalent French scheme, UK consumers may face the prospect of a costly and protracted legal action in the French courts.
>
> (Consumers in the European Community Group 1992: 8)

Nor is it clear that EC legislation gives consumers a higher degree of protection than they would otherwise have received from their own national laws. For example, the 1986 EC Consumer Credit Directive gave consumers in all Member States protection when making purchases on credit, but the UK's existing 1974 Consumer Credit Act already gave consumers a higher level of protection.

Only time will tell whether the SEM will prove beneficial to financial service consumers. However, the signs so far tend to indicate that the social relations between producers and consumers which already exist in Britain will remain intact.

## CONCLUSION

It is clearly the case that financial service producers in Britain have become more consumer orientated. However, it would be inaccurate to conceptualise these trends as a reformulation of the producer–consumer relationship whereby consumers have become more powerful than producers, as some commentators have argued is the case. The number of financial institutions from which consumers can purchase services has declined. The number of bank and building society branches has also fallen in recent years as producers have viewed this area of operations as a prime target for cost cutting. Information technology has also given producers an important method of controlling consumer behaviour via credit referencing and credit scoring.

Similarly, the advent of the Single European Market has been heralded as of infinite benefit for consumers both in terms of providing wider choice and reducing prices. However, a number of reservations have been expressed in relation to the projected reduction in costs and the proposed time scale. There are also a considerable number of factors which may prevent a truly integrated SEM for financial services. These include differences in culture, consumer loyalty to existing producers and the reputational advantages held by domestic producers. Consumer protection was given a low priority by the Commission in the lead up to the SEM. Much more emphasis was paid to the needs and wants of producers. Rather than investment and policies being developed to strengthen existing consumer protection activities, in the likely event that cross-border trade may increase the number and complexity of consumer complaints, funds have been cut. The lack of emphasis on consumer issues has been reflected in the inadequate and disorganised state of redress procedures available to financial service consumers. This is a serious state of affairs. Consumers in Britain have already witnessed the collapse of the Bank of Credit and Commerce International and the Maxwell pension fund scandal. Similar events on a pan-European scale would be nothing short of a monumental disaster.

## SUMMARY

There is little to suggest that the power relations between producers and consumers has significantly altered in Britain since the 1980s. A number of points tend to support this viewpoint:

1 the ability of consumers to chose from a wide-range of financial institutions is more limited than ever before;
2 many financial institutions are closing branches rather than providing a more extensive service for consumers;
3 information technology has presented financial service institutions with a powerful method of consumer surveillance;
4 while the Single European Market has been presented as a considerable advantage for consumers, the projected benefits for consumers have been overestimated.

# Appendix

Northbank is a British retail bank. It was a condition of the research that the bank should remain anonymous. The case study was undertaken in 1990, in three of the bank's branches in the north of England. All of the staff within the three branches and their sub-branches were invited to fill in a self-completion questionnaire. In the event, fifty questionnaires were returned. The completed questionnaires were an accurate reflection of the grade of employees, and the gender distribution of employees in the branches as a whole. Semi-structured interviews were also undertaken with clerical employees and a range of managers: branch, operations, area operations, area personnel, small business and corporate. In all, forty-eight clerical employees and fourteen managers were interviewed. The interviews lasted between thirty and sixty minutes and took place on bank premises.

# Bibliography

Aaker, D.A. and Day, G.S. (1974) 'A Guide to Consumerism', in Aaker, D.A. and Day, G.S. (eds), *Consumerism*, New York: Free Press.

Abercrombie, N. (1991) 'The Privilege of the Producer', in Keat, R. and Abercrombie, N. (eds), *Enterprise Culture*, London: Routledge.

Advisory, Conciliation and Arbitration Service (1988) *Labour Flexibility in Britain: The 1987 ACAS Survey*, Occasional Paper 41.

Albrecht, R. and Zemke, R. (1985) *Service America: Doing Business in the New Economy*, Homewood, Illinois: Dow Jones-Irwin.

Association for Payment Clearing Services (1987) *APACS Review 1986–1987*, London: APACS.

—— (1988) *Research Brief: 1988 Money Transmission Volumes Outlook*, London: APACS.

—— (1989) *Consumer Payments and Financial Behaviour*, London: APACS.

—— (1992) *Consumer Payments and Financial Behaviour*, London: APACS.

Atkinson, J. (1984) 'Manpower Strategies for Flexible Organisations', *Personnel Management*, August, pp. 28–31.

Austrin, T. (1990) 'Financial Retailing: Flexibility, Surveillance and Hype in the New Financial Services Industry', paper presented at the 8th Annual Labour Process Conference, Aston University, Birmingham.

*The Banker* (1988) 'Back Stage Back-Up', May, p. 43.

Banking, Insurance and Finance Union (1988) *Performance Related Pay*, London: BIFU.

Banking Ombudsman Scheme (1991–2), *Annual Report 1991–1992*, London: Office of the Banking Ombudsman.

*Banking Technology* (1989) 'Finding the Right Site', April, pp. 30–2.

*Bank of England Quarterly Bulletin* (1989) 'The Housing Market', 29, 1, pp. 66–77.

Banks, R. (1990) 'Money Management for the Mature: Their Needs and the Services Competing to Meet Them', *Admap*, March, pp. 26–9.

Bartos, R. (1989) *Marketing To Women*, Oxford: Heinemann.

Bateson, J.E.G. (1992) *Managing Services Marketing*, Orlando: Dryden Press.

Battelle Institute (1989) *ATMs Cash Dispensers: An International Survey and Analysis*, London: Battelle Institute.

Benady, A. (1993) 'Tactical Switch by First Direct', *Marketing*, 14 October, p. 13.

Berry, L.L. and Parasuraman, A. (1991) *Marketing Services*, New York: Free Press.

Berry, L.L. and Thompson, T.W. (1982) 'Relationship Banking: The Art of Turning Customers into Clients', *Journal of Retail Banking*, IV, 2, pp. 64–73.

Berry, L.L., Bennett, D.R. and Brown, C.W. (1989) *Service Quality: A Profit Strategy for Financial Institutions*, Homewood, Illinois: Dow Jones-Irwin.

Berry, L.L., Futrell, C.M. and Bowers, M. (1985) *Bankers Who Sell: Improving Selling Effectiveness In Banking*, Homewood, Illinois: Dow Jones-Irwin.

Berthoud, R. and Hinton, T. (1989) *Credit Unions*, London: Pinter Publishers.

Berthoud, R. and Kempson, E. (1992) *Credit and Debt: the PSI Report*, London: Policy Studies Institute.

Bertrand, O. and Noyelle, T. (1988) *Human Resources and Corporate Strategy*, Paris: OECD.

Bitner, M.J. (1992) 'Servicescapes: The Impact of Physical Surroundings on Customers and Employees', *Journal of Marketing*, 56, pp. 57–71.

Blackett, T. (1991) 'The Nature of Brands', in Murphy, J. (ed.), *Brand Valuation*, London: Business Books.

Blair, M. (1991) *Financial Services: The New Core Rules*, London: Blackstone Press.

Bliss, M. (1988) 'The Impact of Retailers on Financial Services', *Long Range Planning*, 21, 1, pp. 55–58.

Booker, J. (1991) *Temples of Mammon*, Edinburgh: Edinburgh University Press.

Bowen, D.E. and Schneider, B. (1985) 'Boundary Spanning-Role Employees and the Service Encounter: Some Guidelines for Management and Research', in Czepiel, J.A., Soloman, M.R. and Surprenant, C.F. (eds), *The Service Encounter: Managing Employee/Customer Interaction in Service Businesses*, Lexington, MA: Lexington Books.

Breeze, E., Trevor, G. and Wilmot, A. (1991) *General Household Survey*, No. 20, London: HMSO.

British Bankers' Association (1992) *Annual Abstract of Statistics*, Vol. 9, London: British Bankers Association.

—— (1993) *Annual Abstract of Statistics*, Vol. 10, London: British Bankers' Association.

Broker, G. (1990) *Competition in Banking*, Paris: OECD.

Brown, A. (1991) *Customer Care Management*, Oxford: Butterworth Heinemann.

Browne, A.H. (1991) 'The Banks and Personal Credit', *Banking World*, January, pp. 17–20.

Buck, S. (1990) 'Turning an Old Problem into a New Opportunity', *Admap*, March, pp. 21–5.

Building Society Ombudsman Scheme (1992–3), *Annual Report 1992–1993*, London: Office of the Building Society Ombudsman.

Burke, T., Maddock, S. and Rose, A. (1993) *How Ethical is British Business?*, Research Working Paper Series 2, No. 1, Faculty of Business, Management and Social Studies, University of Westminster.

Burrows, R. and Marsh. C. (eds), (1992) *Consumption and Class*, London: Macmillan.

Burton, D. (1990) 'Competition in the UK Retail Financial Service Sector: Some Implications for the Spatial Distribution and Function of Bank Branches', *The Service Industries Journal*, 10, 3, pp. 571–88.

—— (1991) 'Tellers into Sellers', *International Journal of Bank Marketing*, 9, 6, pp. 25–9.

—— (1992) 'Banks Go To Market', unpublished PhD thesis, Lancaster University.

Buswell, D. (1986) 'The Development of a Quality Measurement System for a UK Bank', in Moores, B.(ed.), *Are They Being Served*, Oxford: Philip Allan.

Buzzell, R.D. and Gale, B.T. (1987) *The PIMS Principles*, New York: Free Press.

Campbell, C. (1987) *The Romantic Spirit of Modern Consumerism*, Oxford: Basil Blackwell.

Carlzon, J. (1987) *Moments of Truth*, Cambridge, Mass: Ballinger.

Channon, D. (1987) 'The Personal Customer's View', in Chartered Institute of Bankers (eds), *Banking Through The Looking Glass*, London: Chartered Institute of Bankers.

Chrystal, K.A. (1992) 'Don't Shoot the Messenger: Do Banks Deserve the Recent Adverse Publicity?', *National Westminster Bank Quarterly Review*, May, pp. 44–54.

Churchill, G. E. (1972) 'The Marketing Message: the way forward for the insurance industry', *Chartered Insurance Institute Journal*, 69, pp. 153.

Clarke, P.D., Gardener, E.P.M., Feeney, P. and Molyneux, P. (1987) 'Strategic Marketing', *Banking World*, October, pp. 16–20.

—— (1988) 'The Genesis of Strategic Marketing Control in British Retail Banking', *International Journal of Bank Marketing*, 6, 2, pp. 5–19.

Collard, R. and Dale, B. (1985) 'Quality Circles: why they break down and why they hold up', *Personnel Management*, February, pp. 28–31.

Collins, M. (1991) *Banks and Industrial Finance in Britain 1800–1939*, Basingstoke: Macmillan.

Committee of London and Scottish Bankers (1988), *Annual Abstract of Banking Statistics*, Vol. 5, London: CLSB.

Consumers' Association (1992) 'Banking Rights', *Which?*, March, p. 172.

—— (1993) 'Banking From Home', *Which?*, April, pp. 44–7.

Consumers in the European Community Group (1991) *European Consumer Policy*, Briefing Paper 27, London: CECG.

—— (1992) *EC Framework for Financial Services*, Briefing Paper 1, London: CECG.

Co-operative Bank (1992) The Co-operative Bank Puts ethics into Banking, Co-operative Bank, May.

Cowell, D.W. (1984) The Marketing of Services, London: Heinemann.

Crompton, R. and Sanderson, K. (1990) *Gendered Jobs and Social Change*, London: Unwin Hyman.

Crosby, P. (1985) *The Quality Man*, London: BBC Education and Training.

Dale, B. (1986) 'Experience with Quality Circles and Quality Costs', in Moores, B. (ed.), *Are They Being Served*, Oxford: Philip Allan.

De Moubray, G. (1985) 'Staff Contact are the Key', *The Banker*, June, pp. 44–9.

—— (1991) 'Banking is Not Like Selling Toothpaste', *Long Range Planning*, 24, 5, pp. 68–74.

Ditchburn, B. (1990) 'Financial Service Marketing: the corporation as adjective', *Admap*, June, pp. 18–21.

Dixon, R. (1991) *Banking in Europe*, London: Routledge.

Doyle, P. and Seekamp, G. (1989) 'From the Cradle to the Grave: Banks

Discover Age-Segmented Marketing', *Retail Banker International*, 24 April, pp. 9–10.

Drake, L. (1989) *The Building Society Industry in Transition*, Basingstoke: Macmillan.

*The Economist* (1989a) 'Why Saying Yes Isn't Enough', 3 June, pp. 116–18.

*The Economist* (1989b) 'Bankers Learn a Smile on their Face Puts a Buck in their Pocket', 15 July, pp. 87–8.

Edgett, S. and Thwaites, D. (1990) 'The Influence of Environmental Change on the Marketing Practices of Building Societies', *European Journal of Marketing*, 24, 12, pp. 35–47.

Ellinger, B. (1940) *The City*, Westminster: P.S. King and Staples Limited.

Ellwood, P. (1989) 'Lessons and Opportunities in the UK – Barclays Bank', 2nd International Bank Card Conference, *Cards for All: Plastic Democracy in Europe?*, Frankfurt, 9–10 February, London: Lafferty.

Emerson, M. (ed.) (1988) 'The Economics of 1992', *European Economy*, WP No. 35, March, Brussels: EEC.

Ennew, C.T. (1992) 'Consumer Attitudes to Independent Financial Advice', *International Journal of Bank Marketing*, 10, 5, pp. 13–18.

Ennew, C.T. and McKechnie, S. (1992) 'Green Marketing: Can the Banks Respond?', *Marketing Intelligence and Planning*, 10, 7, pp. 8–9.

Ennew, C.T. and Wright, M. (1990) 'Retail Banks and Organisational Change: Evidence from the UK', *International Journal of Bank Marketing*, 8, 1, pp. 4–9.

Equal Opportunities Commission (1986) *Sex Equality and Credit Scoring*, Manchester: EOC.

—— (1988) *Credit for Women*, Manchester: EOC.

—— (1989a) *A Sound Investment? The Treatment of Women by Financial Institutions*, London: HMSO.

—— (1989b) *Counter Discrimination*, Manchester: EOC.

—— (1992) *Your Pension Matters*, Manchester: EOC.

Etkins, P. (1992) 'Ethical Banking', in Reifner, U. and Ford, J. (eds), *Banking for People*, Berlin: Walter de Gruyter.

Euromonitor (1992) *Consumer Banking and Personal Finance in Europe 1992*, London: Euromonitor.

Evans, W. (1988) 'Housing Finance in Europe', *Chartered Building Society Institute Journal*, 41, 185, pp. 202–4.

Fernstrom, M.M. (1989) 'Consumer Education: New Directions', *The Credit World*, 77, 6, pp. 18–24.

FIET (1984) *The Future of the Branch Network in Banking*, Switzerland: FIET.

—— (1987) *Part-Time Work in Financial Institutions: An International Trade Union Enquiry*, Switzerland: FIET.

*Financial Times* (1989) 'Survey: Plastic Cards', 6 December.

—— (1990a) 'Access Loses Lloyds 375,000 Cardholders', 1 February.

—— (1990b) 'Barclays £8 Fee Aims to Halt Decline in Profits', 25 April.

Folly, M.J. (1990) 'Retaining Customer Loyalty in an Increasingly Competitive Market', *International Journal of Bank Marketing*, 8, 3, pp. 17–24.

Ford, J. (1988) *The Indebted Society*, London: Routledge.

—— (1991) *Consuming Credit: Debt and Poverty in the UK*, London: Child Poverty Action Group.

—— (1992) 'Mortgage Arrears: prospects for the 1990s' *Chartered Building Society Institute Journal*, January, pp. 11–12.

Ford, R. (1990) 'Insurance Advertising in the 1990s', *Admap*, June, pp. 22–5.

Fortescue, S.H. (1987) 'Financial Deregulation – How is it Affecting UK Banks?', *Financial Products and Banking Services Delivery Strategies for Tomorrow*, Prague: European Finance Management and Marketing Association, 15–18 November.

Fox, A. (1985) *Man Mismanagement*, London: Hutchinson.

Fuller, L. and Smith, V. (1991) 'Consumers' Reports: Management by Consumers in a Changing Economy', *Work, Employment and Society*, 5, 1, pp. 1–16.

Gardener, C. and Sheppard, J. (1989) *Consuming Passion*, London: Unwin Hyman.

Gardener, E.P.M. (1992) 'Banking Strategies and 1992', in Mullineux, A. (ed.), *European Banking*, Oxford: Basil Blackwell.

Gavaghan, K. (1988) 'The Advertising of Personal Financial Services by the Banks', *Financial Communications and Advertising Conference*, 11–12 May.

—— (1990) 'To Market to Market....', *Banking World*, March, pp. 16–20.

George, W. and Berry, L. (1981) 'Guidelines for the Advertising of Services', *Business Horizons*, 24, pp. 53–9.

Gershuny, J. and Miles, I. (1983) *The New Service Economy: The Transformation of Employment in Industrial Societies*, London: Frances Pinter.

Glennie, P.D. and Thrift, N.J. (1992) 'Modernity, Urbanism, and Modern Consumption', *Environment and Planning D: Society and Space*, 10, pp. 423–43.

Gorse, D. (1978) 'Consumers' Association and Which?', in Mitchell, J. (ed.), *Marketing and the Consumer Movement*, London: McGraw-Hill.

Graham, C., Seneviratne, M. and James, R. (1993) 'Publicising the Bank and Building Society Ombudsman Schemes', *Consumer Policy Review*, 3, 2, pp. 85–91.

Graham, N., Beatson, M., Wells, W. (1989) '1977 to 1987: A Decade of Service', *Employment Gazette*, Nos. 45–54.

Green, C.F. (1989) 'Business Ethics in Banking', *Journal of Business Ethics*, 8, pp. 631–4.

Gronmo, S. and Olander, F. (1991) 'Consumer Power: Enabling and Limiting Factors', *Journal of Consumer Policy*, 14, 2, pp. 141–69.

Gronroos, C. (1984) *Strategic Management and Marketing in the Service Sector*, Lund: Studentlitteratur.

—— (1985) 'Internal Marketing-Theory and Practice', in Bloch, T.M., Block, H.R., Upah, G.D., Young and Zeithaml, V.A. (eds), *Services Marketing in a Changing Environment*, Chicago: American Marketing Association.

—— (1990) 'Marketing Redefined', *Management Decision*, 28, 8, pp. 5–9.

*Guardian* (1989) 'Higher Cheque Guarantee Limit', 20 April.

Gummesson, E. (1991) 'Marketing-orientation Revisited: The Crucial Role of the Part-time Marketer', *European Journal of Marketing*, 25, 2, pp. 60–75.

Hall, S. (1988) 'Brave New World', *Marxism Today*, October, pp. 24–9.

Harvey, D. (1989) *The Condition of Postmodernity*, Oxford: Basil Blackwell.

Henderson, G.L. (1992) 'Girobank: The First Bank to Win a British Quality Award', *Quality Forum*, 18, 2, pp. 80–7.

Hirschhorn, L. (1985) 'Information Technology and the New Services Game', in Castells, M. (ed.), *High Technology, Space, and Society*, Beverly Hills: Sage.

HM Treasury (1987) 'Share Ownership in Britain', *Economic Progress Report*, No. 189, April.

—— (1989) 'Trends in Saving', *Economic Progress Report*, No. 200, February.

Hochschild, A.R. (1983) *The Managed Heart: Commercialisation of Human Feelings*, Berkeley, California: University of California Press.

Holmes, M.J. (1992) 'The European Market for Mortgage Finance and 1992', in Mullineux, A. (ed.), *European Banking*, Oxford: Basil Blackwell.

Holton, R.H. (1974) 'Foreword', in Aaker, D.A. and Day, G.S. (eds), *Consumerism*, New York: Free Press.

Hooley, G.J. and Mann, S.J. (1988) 'The Adoption of Marketing By Financial Institutions in the UK', *The Service Industries Journal*, 8, 4, pp. 488–500.

Howcroft, B. (1992) 'Customer Service in Selected Branches of a UK Clearing Bank', *The Service Industries Journal*, 12, 1, pp, 125–42.

Howcroft, J.B. and Hill, C. (1992) 'Customer Service Quality in the Mortgage Market', *Chartered Building Society Institute Journal*, September, pp. 8–12.

Howcroft, J.B. and Lavis, J. (1986) *Retail Banking: The New Revolution in Structure and Strategy*, Oxford: Basil Blackwell.

Howes, K. (1992) 'Debit Cards: The Cost of Fraud', *The Treasurer*, October, pp. 14–16.

*Industrial Relations Review and Report* (1990) 'Cashless Pay: An End to the Weekly Wage Packet?', 20 March, pp. 5–9.

Insurance Ombudsman (1992) *Annual Report 1992*, London: Office of the Insurance Ombudsman.

Inter-Bank Research Organisation (1985) *Research Brief: Consumer Payments and Financial Behaviour*, London: IBRO.

*Investors Chronicle* (1993) 'Ethics Can Pay', 5 March, pp. 16–17.

Irvine, J. (1980) 'Do Little Savers Get Short Changed?', *Sunday Times*, 5 October.

Jack, R. (1992) 'Obligations to Personal Consumers', in *Banks and Their Obligations*, Chartered Institute of Bankers Cambridge Seminar, CIB: London.

Jain, A.K., Pinson, C. and Malhotra, N.K. (1987) 'Customer Loyalty as a Construct in the Marketing of Bank Services', *International Journal of Bank Marketing*, 5, 3, pp. 49–70.

Johnson, P. (1990) 'Economic Trends in Population – last 25 years, next 10 years', *Admap*, March, 14–17.

Jones, C. (1989) 'Defensive Strategies', *The Banker*, October, pp. 72–74.

Kanter, R.M. (1987) 'The Attack on Pay', *Harvard Business Review*, 2, pp. 60–7.

Kay, W. (1987) *Battle for the High Street*, London: Piatkus.

Keat, R. (1991) 'Starship Britain or Universal Enterprise?', in Keat, R. and Abercrombie, N. (eds), *Enterprise Culture*, London: Routledge.

Knights, D. and Morgan, G. (1990) 'Management Control in Sales Forces: A Case Study from the Labour Process of Life Assurance', *Work, Employment and Society*, 4, 3, pp. 369–90.

Kosciusko, J. (1989) 'The Economics of the Debit Card', 2nd International Bank Card Conference, *Cards for All: Plastic Democracy in Europe?*, Frankfurt, 9–10 February, London: Lafferty.

Lamb, A. (1991) *Banking in the European Community After 1992*, London: Chartered Institute of Bankers.

Lamont, N. (1988) 'What Has Been Achieved Through Privatisations', paper given at the Financial Communications and Advertising Conference organised by the *Financial Times*, London, May.

Lane, C. (1987) 'Capitalism or Culture? A Comparative Analysis of the Position in the Labour Market of Lower White-Collar Workers in the Financial Services Sector of Britain and the Federal Republic of Germany', *Work, Employment and Society*, 1, 1, pp. 57–83.

Laurie, S. (1989) 'Putting on the Ritz', *The Banker*, May, pp. 13–15.

Leadbeater, C. (1988) 'Power to the Person', *Marxism Today*, October, pp. 14–19.

Lever, L. (1992) *The Barlow Clowes Affair*, London: Macmillan.

Lewis, B.R. (1982) 'Weekly Cash Paid Workers: Attitudes and Behaviour with Regard to Banks and Other Financial Institutions', *European Journal of Bank Marketing*, 16, 3, pp. 92–101.

—— (1989) 'Quality in the Service Sector: A Review', *International Journal of Bank Marketing*, 7, 5, pp. 4–12.

—— (1991) 'Service Quality: An International Comparison of Bank Customers' Expectations and Perceptions', *Journal of Marketing Management*, 7, pp. 47–62.

Lewis, B.R. and Bingham, G.H. (1991) 'The Youth Market for Financial Services', *International Journal of Bank Marketing*, 9, 2, pp. 3–11.

Lewis, B.R. and Smith, A.M. (1989) 'Customer Care in Financial Service Organisations', *International Journal of Bank Marketing*, 7, 5, pp. 13–22.

Lewis, M.K. and Chiplin, B. (1986) 'Characteristics of Markets for Personal Financial Services', in Carter, R.L. *et al.* (eds), *Personal Financial Markets*, Oxford: Philip Allan.

Llewellyn, D. (1987) 'Competition and the Regulatory Mix', *National Westminster Bank Quarterly Review*, August, pp. 4–13.

—— (1992) 'Banking and Financial Services', in Swann, D. (ed.), *The Single European Market and Beyond*, London: Routledge.

Lomax, D.F. (1987) *London Markets after the Financial Services Act*, London: Butterworths.

MacInnes, J. (1988) 'New Technology in Scotbank: Gender, Class and Work, in Hyman', R. and Streeck, W. (eds), *New Technology and Industrial Relations*, Oxford: Basil Blackwell.

Mahoney, J. (1991) 'Ethical Aspects of Banking', in Chartered Institute of Bankers (eds), *The Banks and Society*, London: Chartered Institute of Bankers.

*Marketing* (1989), 'Banking on Direct Debit', 2 November, p. 3.

—— (1992a) 'Top 500 Brands', April, pp. 22–5.

—— (1992b) 'Midland Listens Harder', July, p. 2.

Marshall, C. (1985) 'Can We Be Consumer-Oriented in a Changing Financial Service World?', *Journal of Consumer Marketing*, 2, 4, pp. 37–43.

Mayers, S. (1991) 'Building a Bank: First Direct', paper given at the European Financial Management and Marketing Association, Brussels, 5–6 February.

Mazey, S. and Richardson, J. (1992) 'British Pressure Groups in the European Community: The Challenge of Brussels', *Parliamentary Affairs*, 45, 1, pp. 92–107.

McGee, A. (1992) *The Financial Service Ombudsmen*, London: Fourmat Publishing.

McIver, C. and Naylor, G. (1980) *Marketing Financial Services*, London: Institute of Bankers.

Meller, P. (1991a) 'Banking On Change', *Marketing*, 21 February, pp. 22–3.

—— (1991b) 'Midland Takes a Simpler Tack', *Marketing*, 8 August, p. 2.

—— (1992), 'Boxing in Your Customers', *Marketing*, 28 May, p. 22.

—— (1993) 'Competition on Price Promotes Insurance Swap', Marketing, 2 September, p. 2.

Mersha, T. and Adlakha, V. (1992) 'Attributes of Service Quality: The Consumers' Perspective', *International Journal of Service Industry Management*, 3, 3, pp. 34–45.

Middleton, P. (1987) 'Are Non-Banks Winning In Retail Financial Services?', *International Journal of Bank Marketing*, 5, 1, pp. 4–18.

Mills, P.K., Chase, R.B. and Margulies, N. (1985) 'Motivating the Client/Employment System as a Service Production Strategy', *Academy of Management Review*, 8, 2, pp. 50–66.

Mitchell, D. (1993) 'Interest Groups and the "Democratic Deficit" ', *European Access*, 2, pp. 14–17.

Mitchell, J. (1978) 'Some Lessons for Marketing' in Mitchell, J. (ed.), *Marketing and the Consumer Movement*, London: McGraw-Hill.

—— (1991a) *Banker's Racket or Consumer Benefit?*, London: Policy Studies Institute.

—— (1991b) 'Ombudsman Schemes – A Consumer View', *Banking World*, June, pp. 22–3.

—— (1992a) 'Obligations to Society', in *Banks and Their Obligations*, Chartered Institute of Bankers Cambridge Seminar, London: CIB.

—— (1992b) 'Savings and Investments Consumer Issues', a report to the Office of Fair Trading, June.

Mitchell, J.W. and Sparks, L. (1988) 'Technology and Bank Marketing Information Systems', *Journal of Marketing Management*, Summer, pp. 50–60.

Morgan, G. and Knights, D. (1992) 'Constructing Consumers and Consumer Protection: the Case of the Life Insurance Industry in the United Kingdom', in Burrows, R. and Marsh, C. (eds), *Consumption and Class*, London: Macmillan.

Murphy, J. (1990) *Brand Strategy*, London: Director Books.

National Consumer Council (1983) *Banking Services and the Consumer*, London: Methuen.

—— (1987) *Credit Card Services: Response to the Monopolies and Mergers Commission Enquiry*, London: NCC.

—— (1990) *Credit and Debit; the Consumer Interest*, London: HMSO.

—— (1991a) *Response on the Draft Directive on Liability for Services*, London: NCC.

—— (1991b) *Extortionate Credit: Response from the National Consumer Council to the Director-General of Fair Trading*, London: NCC.

—— (1991c) *Banking Code of Practice: Response by the National Consumer Council*, London: NCC.

—— (1993a) *Consumer Advice Services in the European Community: A Directory*, London: NCC.

—— (1993b) *Ombudsman Services – Consumers' views of the Office of the*

*Building Societies Ombudsmen and the Insurance Ombudsman Bureau*, London: NCC.

Nevans, R. (1987) *Bankers and Payments The European Perspective*, London: Lafferty Publications.

Newman, K. (1984) *Financial Marketing and Communications*, Eastbourne: Holt, Rinehart and Winston.

Occupational Pensions Advisory Service (1991–2), *Report and Accounts 1991–1992*, London: OPAS.

OECD (1989a) *Plastic Cards and the Consumer*, Paris: OECD.

—— (1989b) *Consumer Policy in OECD Countries 1987–1988*, Paris: OECD.

Office of Fair Trading (1987) *The Financial Intermediaries, Managers and Brokers Regulatory Association*, London: Office of Fair Trading.

—— (1991) *Annual Consumer Complaints Survey 1990: Findings on Redress*, London: Office of Fair Trading.

—— (1992a) *Independent Financial Advisors and the Impact of Commission Disclosure*, London: Office of Fair Trading.

—— (1992b) *Credit Scoring*, London: Office of Fair Trading.

O'Reilly, J. (1992) 'Banking on Flexibility: A Comparison of the Use of Flexible Employment Strategies in the Retail Banking Sector in Britain and France', *The International Journal of Human Resource Management*, 3, 1, pp. 35–58.

Otley, D. (1991) *United Bank: A case study of the Implementation of a Performance-Related Reward Scheme*, Departmental Paper, Department of Accounting and Finance, The Management School, Lancaster University.

Parasuraman, A., Zeithaml, V.A. and Berry, L.L. (1985) 'A Conceptual Model of Service Quality and its Implications for Future Research', *Journal of Marketing*, Fall, pp. 41–50.

Parker, G. (1990) *Getting and Spending; Credit and Debt in Britain*, Aldershot: Avebury

Penn, V. (1991) 'Retail EFTPOS 90: Paper Holds Out Against Plastic', *International Journal of Retail and Distribution Management*, January/February, pp. 10–12.

*Personnel Management* (1992) 'Using Incentives to Reward and Motivate Employees', pp. 49–52.

Porter, L.W. and Lawler, E.E. (1968) *Managerial Attitudes and Performance*, London: Irwin.

Rajan, A. (1987a) 'New Technology and Career Progression in Financial Institutions', *Service Industries Journal*, 7, 1, pp. 35–40.

—— (1987b) *Services – The Second Industrial Revolution?*, London: Butterworth.

Rajan, A. and Cooke, G. (1986) 'The Impact of Information Technology on Employment in the Financial Services Industry', *National Westminster Bank Quarterly Review*, August, pp. 21–35.

Rathmell, J. (1974) *Marketing in the Service Sector*, Cambridge: Winthrop Publishers.

Read, C.N. (1982) 'The Implications of Technological Change', paper presented to the 35th International Banking Summer School, 16 June 1982, at St Andrew's University, Scotland.

Reichheld, F.F. and Sasser, W.E. (1990) 'Zero Defections: Quality Comes to Services', *Harvard Business Review*, September–October, pp. 105–111.

Reifner, U. and Ford, J. (1992) *Banking for People*, Berlin: Walter de Gruyter.

*Retail Banker International* (1989) 'US Banks Discover Wealth in the Grey Market', 24 April, p. 11.

Review Committee On Banking Services Law (1990) *Banking Services Law and Practice*, Report by the Review Committee, London: HMSO.

Robinson, D. (1982) 'IT and Banking Systems', *Journal of the Institute of Bankers*, June.

Robinson, O. (1985) 'The Changing Labour Market: The Phenomenon of Part-Time Employment', *National Westminster Bank Quarterly Review*, pp. 19–29.

Russell, T. (1975) *The Economics of the Credit Card*, New York: Prager.

Salway, S.J. (1989) 'The Battle of the School Leavers', *The Scottish Banker*, May, pp. 6–7.

Saunders, P. (1990) *A Nation of Home Owners*, London: Unwin Hyman.

Shapiro, B.P., Rangan, V.K., Moriarty, R.T. and Ross, E.B. (1987) 'Manage Customers for Profits (Not Just Sales)', *Harvard Business Review*, 5, pp. 101–8.

Shelton, D.W. (1990) 'Impact of Financial Services Act on Investment Products', *International Journal of Bank Marketing*, 8, 2, pp. 12–16.

Shurman, L. (1991) 'What is Fair in the Relationship Between a Bank and its Customer?', in the Chartered Institute of Bankers (eds), *The Banks and Society*, London: The Chartered Institute of Bankers.

Singh, J. and Pandya, S. (1991) 'Exploring the Effects of Consumers' Dissatisfaction Level on Complaint Behaviours', *European Journal of Marketing*, 25, 9, pp. 7–21.

Sivanandan, A. (1989) 'All that Melts into Air is Solid: the Hokum of New Times', *Race and Class*, 31, 3, pp. 1–30.

Sleight, P. (1992) 'Where they Live: UK Geodemographic Systems in 1992', *Admap*, May, pp. 17–22.

Smith, A.M. and Lewis, B.R. (1989) 'Customer Care in Financial Service Organisations', *International Journal of Bank Marketing*, 7, 5, pp. 13–22.

*Social Trends* (1989) No. 21, London: HMSO.

—— (1992) No. 24, London: HMSO.

Soloman, M.R. (1992) *Consumer Behaviour*, Boston: Allyn and Bacon.

Standen, J. (1988) 'Have Privatisations Changed the Rules for the Rest of the Market?', *Financial Communications and Advertising Conference*, May, London.

Surprenant, C.F. and Solomon, M.R. (1985) 'Dimensions of Personalization', in Bloch *et al.*, *Services Marketing in a Changing Environment*, USA: American Marketing Association.

Swan, J.E. and Coombs, L.J. (1976) 'Product Performance and Consumer Satisfaction: A New Concept', *Journal of Marketing*, 40, p. 2.

Swann, D. (1979) *Competition and Consumer Protection*, Harmondsworth: Penguin.

Tarver, J.L. (1987) 'In Search of a Competitive Edge in Banking: A Personnel Approach', *The International Journal of Bank Marketing*, 5, 1, pp. 61–8.

Taylor, R. (1987) 'The Branding of Services' in Murphy, J.M. (ed.), *Branding: A Key Marketing Tool*, Basingstoke: Macmillan.

Thomas, R. and Weatherill, S. (1991) 'Consumer Regulation Across Borders', *Consumer Policy Review*, 1, 1, pp. 13–20.

Thomson, H. (1986) 'Customer Loyalty Counts for Less', *The Banker*, July, pp. 30–3.
—— (1992a) 'Are We Playing the Wrong Tune to the People Who Pay the Piper?', *Scottish Banker*, February, pp. 4–5.
—— (1992b) 'Yorkshire Finds Schools the Key to Expansion', *The Scottish Banker*, May, pp. 9–10.
—— (1992c) 'Chasing the Increasingly Footloose Customer', *The Scottish Banker*, August, pp. 6–7.
Thompson, T.W., Berry, L.L. and Donnelly, J.M. (1985) 'The Marketing/Retail Banking Partnership: An Evolutionary Perspective', *Journal of Retail Banking*, 7, 2, pp. 9–22.
Trebilcock, M.J. (1991) 'Taking Stock: Consumerism in the 1990s', *Canadian Business Law Journal*, 19, pp. 412–36.
Turnbull, P.W and Wootton, I.J. (1980) 'The Bank Manager: Marketeer, Salesman or Administrator', *European Journal of Marketing*, 14, 8, pp. 471–92.
Turner, P., Dale, I. and Hurst, C. (1992) 'Training – A Key to the Future', *Employment Gazette*, August, 379–85.
Urry, J. (1986) 'Some Social and Spatial Aspects of Services', *Environment and Planning* D, 5, 1, pp. 5–26.
—— (1990) 'Work, Production and Social Relations', *Work, Employment and Society*, 4, 2, pp. 271–80.
van der Merwe, S. (1987) 'Deregulation in Services and the Marketing Challenge', *Service Industries Journal*, 7, 1, pp. 24–34.
Vickers, J. and Yarrow, G. (1988) *Privatisation: An Economic Analysis*, Cambridge, Mass: MIT.
Vittas, D. and Frazer, P. (1982) *The Retail Banking Revolution*, London: Lafferty.
Vogler, H. (1992) 'Financial Services – Who will Gain from the Single Market?', in Reifner, U. and Ford, J. (eds), *Banking for People*, Berlin: Walter de Gruyter.
Waldrop, J. (1991) 'Educating the Customer', *American Demographics*, 13, 9, pp. 44–7.
Watanabe, T. (1990) 'New Office Technology in Japanese Banking', *New Technology, Work and Employment*, 5, 1, pp. 56–66.
Watkins, J. (1992) 'Information Systems: in the UK retail financial services sector', *Marketing Intelligence and Planning*, 10, 6, pp. 13–17.
Watkins, T. (1990) 'Insurance Marketing', in Ennew, C., Watkins, T. and Wright, M. (eds), *Marketing Financial Services*, Oxford: Heinemann.
Watkins, T. and Wright, M. (1986) *Marketing Financial Services*, London: Butterworths.
Watson, I.J. (1982) 'The Adoption of Marketing By the English Clearing Banks', *European Journal of Marketing*, 16, 3, pp. 23–30.
Whelan, S. (1989) 'Bank's Direct Line to the Future', *Marketing*, pp. 25–6.
Whysall, P. (1989) 'Services Uses in a Major Shopping Centre: Change in Nottingham', *The Service Industries Journal*, 9, 3, pp. 420–38.
Wiesner, H. (1992) *Savings and Investments Consumer Issues*, report to the Office of Fair Trading.
Williams, C. (1988) *Blue, White and Pink Collar Workers in Australia*, London: Allen & Unwin.

Worthington, S. (1992) 'Plastic Cards and Consumer Credit', *International Journal of Retail and Distribution Management*, 20, 7, pp. 3–9.

York, D.A. and Hayes, A. (1982) 'Working Females as a Market Segment', *European Journal of Bank Marketing*, 16, 3, pp. 83–91.

# Name index

Aaker, D.A. and Day, G.S. 81
Abercrombie, N. 3, 25
ACAS 60
Albrecht, R. and Zemke, R. 47
Association for Payment Clearing
    Services (APACS) 1, 8, 12, 13,
    68–70, 77
Atkinson, J. 60
Austrin, T. 49

*The Banker* 30
*Bank of England Quarterly Bulletin* 21
Banking, Insurance and Finance
    Union 61
Banking Ombudsman 89
*Banking Technology* 42
Banks, R. 14
Bartos, R. 11
Bateson, J.E.G. 40–1
Battelle Institute 70
Benady, A. 75
Berry, L.L. and Futrell, C.M. 53
Berry, L.L. and Parasuraman, A. 51,
    58
Berry, L.L. and Thompson, T.W. 53
Berry, L.L., Bennett, D.R. and Brown
    C.W. 28, 51
Berthoud, R. and Hinton, T. 17
Berthoud, R. and Kempson, E. 16, 19
Bertrand, O. and Noyelle, T. 50, 52
Bitner, M.J. 40
Blackett, T. 38
Blair, M. 85–6
Bliss, M. 72
Booker, J. 41

Bowen, D.E. and Schneider, B. 55
Breeze, E., Trevor, G. and Wilmot,
    A. 20
British Bankers' Association 1, 16,
    20, 71–2, 77, 100
Broker, G. 106
Brown, A. 47
Browne, A.H. 96
Building Society Ombudsman 91
Burke, T., Maddock, S. and Rose, A. 95
Burrows, R. and Marsh, C. 2
Burton, D. 10, 56–8, 62–3, 100–1
Buswell, D. 49
Buzzell, R.D. and Gale, B.T. 50

Campbell, C. 24–5
Carlzon, J. 47
Channon, D. 37, 49
Chrystal, K.A. 2
Churchill, G.E. 35
Clarke, P.D., Gardener, E.P.M.,
    Feeney, P. and Molyneux, P. 27,
    30, 35
Co-operative Bank 37–8
Collard, R. and Dale, B. 54
Collins, M. 99
Committee of London and Scottish
    Bankers 13, 100
Consumers' Association 95
Consumers in the European
    Community Group 106, 108,
    110–11
Cowell, D.W. 40
Crompton, R. and Sanderson, K. 59,
    101

Crosby, P. 51

Dale, B. 54
de Moubray, G. 28, 33
Ditchburn, B. 33
Dixon, R. 105
Doyle, P. and Seekamp, G. 14
Drake, L. 99

*The Economist* 28, 48
Edgett, S. and Thwaites, D. 29
Ellinger, B. 34
Ellwood, P. 38, 72
Emerson, M. 13, 104
Ennew, C. T. 76
Ennew, C.T. and McKechnie, S. 38
Ennew, C.T. and Wright, M. 74
Equal Opportunities Commission 11
Etkins, P. 95
Euromonitor 105
Evans, W. 19

Fernstrom, M.M. 84
FIET 100–1
*Financial Times* 36, 70, 73
Folly, M.J. 65
Ford, J. 17, 21, 29, 34
Fortescue, S.H. 18
Fox, A. 60
Fuller, L. and Smith V. 60

Gardener, E.P.M. 104–5
Gardener, C. and Sheppard, J. 25–6
Gavaghan, K. 23, 28
George, W. and Berry, L. 33
Gershuny, J. and Miles, I. 47
Glennie, P.D. and Thrift, N.J. 3
Gorse, D. 83, 94
Graham, C., Seneviratne, M. and
  James, R. 93
Graham, N., Beatson, M., Wells, W.
  10
Gronmo, S. and Olander, F. 83
Gronroos, C. 55, 58
*Guardian* 77
Gummesson, E. 55

Hall, S. 2
Harvey, D. 2, 35

Henderson, G.L. 51
Hirschhorn, L. 52
HM Treasury 22
Hochschild, A.R. 49
Holmes, M.J. 19, 105
Holton, R.H. 82
Hooley, G.J. and Mann, S.J. 28
Howcroft, B. 57
Howcroft, J.B. and Hill, C. 50
Howcroft, J.B. and Lavis, J. 42
Howes, K. 78

*Industrial Relations Review and
  Report* 13
Insurance Ombudsman 89
Inter-Bank Research Organisation 70
*Investors Chronicle* 38
Irvine, J. 15

Jack, R. 82–3, 87
Jain, A.K., Pinson, C. and Malhotra,
  N.K. 68
Johnson, P. 13–14
Jones, C. 106

Kanter, R.M. 60
Kay, W. 41, 44
Keat, R. 3, 26, 99
Knights, D. and Morgan, G. 62
Kosciusko, J. 72

Lamb, A. 110
Lamont, N. 21
Lane, C. 53
Laurie, S. 74
Leadbeater, C. 1, 2
Lever, L. 85
Lewis, B.R. 12, 15, 18, 46–8
Lewis, B.R. and Bingham, G.H. 68
Lewis, B.R. and Smith, A.M. 47
Lewis, M.K. and Chiplin, B.
Llewellyn, D. 84, 104, 106
Lomax, D.F. 85

MacInnes, J. 101
Mahoney, J. 96
*Marketing* 32–3, 52, 71
Marshall, C. 60
Mayers, S. 74

# Subject index

Abbey National 27, 30
ACAS 60
account holding 1, 4; children 5, 15; dual 5, 67–9; explanation of 8–10; France 67; manual workers 12–13; socio-economic group 8; students 15–16; women 8, 10–12; young people 8, 68–9
accounts, multi-service 36
ACORN 37
advertising 4–6, 21, 24, 31–5
American Express 83–4
anti-consumption 77
atmospherics 40
automated payments 5–6, 12–13
automatic teller machines 9, 36, 43, 49, 69–70, 74, 100

BACS 71
Bank of Credit and Commerce International (BCCI) 86, 112
Bank of England 41
Bank of Scotland 38
Banking Code 87
Banking Information Service 31
Banking, Insurance and Finance Union 61, 63
Banking Ombudsman 89–90
banks (see under name)
Barclaycard 72
Barclays Bank 31–2, 73
Barlow Clowes 86
branches: decline of 99–100; image 4, 41; listed building status 43; location 42, 100; zoning 43–4

branding 4, 38–9
British Airways 22
British Gas 22
British Petroleum 22
British Telecom 22
building societies (see under name)
Building Societies Ombudsman Scheme 90–1
Bureau Européen des Unions de Consommateurs 108

cash 12–13
cashless pay 12–13
cashless payments 12–13
cashless society 69–72
Cecchini Report 102–7
charges 35, 52, 61, 83
cheques 71–2
cheque cards 71–2, 77
Citizens' Advice Bureaux 81
Classic account 16, 35
clerical employees 56–9, 63
Coca Cola 39
Code of Banking Practice 2, 94–5
commission 52, 61, 83
complaining behaviour: dissatisfaction 51; ombudsmen schemes 93
Confederation of Family Organisations in the European Community 108–9
Connect 78
consumer: education 83–4; enterprising 26; groups 1; inertia 67; loyalty 14–15, 51–2, 66–9;